The Proverbs Explained

Fr. Mitch Pacwa, S.J.

THE PROVERBS EXPLAINED

A Blueprint for Christian Living

EWTN PUBLISHING, INC.
Irondale, Alabama

EWTN Publishing, Inc.
5817 Old Leeds Road, Irondale, AL 35210

Distributed by Sophia Institute Press, Box 5284, Manchester, NH 03108

Library of Congress Cataloging-in-Publication Data

Names: Pacwa, Mitch, 1949- author.
Title: The Proverbs explained : a blueprint for Christian living / Fr. Mitch Pacwa, S.J.
Description: Irondale, Alabama : EWTN Publishing, Inc., 2017.
Identifiers: LCCN 2017000610 | ISBN 9781682780268 (pbk. : alk. paper)
Subjects: LCSH: Bible. Proverbs—Criticism, interpretation, etc.
Classification: LCC BS1465.52 .P33 2017 | DDC 223/.706—dc23 LC record available at https://lccn.loc.gov/2017000610

To Tim Brown, a lover of Proverbs who worked with Mother Angelica from the beginning and helped produce the Proverbs series on which this book was based

Contents

Part 3

Virtue

The Proverbs Explained

Introduction

"Wisdom! Let us be attentive!" In the Byzantine Divine Liturgy of St. John Chrysostom the deacon or priest makes this proclamation to the congregation before the first reading from the epistles, and again before the Gospel. St. John Chrysostom was the Patriarch of Constantinople when that city's cathedral was the first Hagia Sophia Church, a name meaning "Holy Wisdom." Both the name of that famous cathedral and the proclamation of the Byzantine liturgy bring out the importance of wisdom for Christians.

This great respect for wisdom did not begin with Christians, by any means; the Old Testament includes a number of wisdom books: Job, Ecclesiastes, Sirach, and, of course, the book of Wisdom, and many other books, especially the Psalms, contain the wisdom of history and of the prophets. Wisdom is an important component of all of Scripture, and this is reflected in that proclamation in the Byzantine liturgy.

The book of Proverbs is one of these wisdom books; indeed, it may be the model for the wisdom of Israel. It is a collection of wise teachings that was composed throughout the history of Israel, as the book indicates. For instance, the beginnings of chapters 1, 10, and 25 identify collections of instructions and proverbs that are attributed to Solomon. In the Bible, wisdom is frequently connected with Solomon: before dying, David addresses Solomon as "a wise man" (1 Kings 2:9); Solomon prayed that God would give him understanding so that he might be a just king, so the Lord granted him wisdom (1 Kings 3:3–14). More directly, Solomon is credited with the composition of many proverbs and songs (1 Kings 4:32). Because of his renown for wisdom, much of the book of Proverbs came to be associated with this great king.

The book also mentions authors of proverbs other than Solomon, however: "the words of the wise" (22:17 — 24:22); "these are also sayings of the wise" (24:23–34); "the words of Agur, son of Jakeh of Massa" (30:1–33); and "the words of Lemuel, king of Massa" (31:1–9). The editors of Proverbs preserved traces of their process of collecting wisdom sayings of different people from different periods of history, and these differences are confirmed by the different writing styles throughout the book, which are especially apparent in the original Hebrew. The collection process probably began during Solomon's reign and continued throughout the history of the Judahite monarchy and perhaps after the Babylonian exile.

This makes it difficult to date any particular saying. The most reliable historical reference point is an explicit mention of the king, which probably dates a proverb to the monarchic period. Proverbs about general human experiences, however, cannot be dated with certainty. In fact, a key to the genius of wisdom is that it transcends any particular period or culture and applies to wise people throughout history.

Forms of Speech in Proverbs

The teachers of wisdom, known as sages, mostly used two forms of speech in their teaching: the proverb and the instruction. The more common form is the proverb, which takes shape as two succinct parallel phrases. The thesis of a proverb is based on experience, and so anyone who examines life can confirm its truth; and it lacks explicit commands, so as to allow the readers or listeners to draw their own conclusions for their behavior. These statements are full of the anticipation of taking some action, but part of the training in wisdom is to induce the student to come to a good conclusion on his own by taking wise action. Of course, if the student does not take the appropriate action, he remains a fool. This is one of the ways the proverbs are meant to teach us.

There are different subtypes of proverbs that are determined by the kind of parallelism found in each one. The most common type of parallelism is *antithetic*, where the first statement is balanced by a contrasting statement:

> Treasures of wickedness do not profit, but righteousness delivers from death. (Prov. 10:2)

A second type of proverb is the *synthetic* parallel, presenting an image in the first line and its resolution in the second:

> Take away the dross from the silver, and the smith has material for a vessel; take away the wicked from the presence of the king, and his throne will be established in righteousness. (Prov. 25:4–5)

A third type of proverb is the synonymous parallel, in which two phrases repeat each other's thought in slightly different form:

> It is not good to be partial to a wicked man, or to deprive a righteous man of justice. (Prov. 18:5)

The second form of speech is the instruction, which is typically a longer, more developed unit that seeks to motivate its hearers to action. Typically a teacher addresses the student as "my son" to establish a relational claim upon him. He often uses the imperative mood, commanding the student to choose the correct way of action and avoid the evil way leading to destruction. We find the instructions are collected mostly in Proverbs 1–9.

The Structure and Dating of Proverbs

The book of Proverbs contains eight major units, based on differences in forms of speech and editorial divisions.

1. "The Proverbs of Solomon" (1–9) are a series of undatable instructions.

2. "The Proverbs of Solomon" (10:1–22:16) are a series of mostly antithetic proverbs. These proverbs cannot be dated, although the presence of Aramaisms, that is, Aramaic words that are included in the Hebrew text (14:34; 16:10; 18:24; 19:20; and others), may point to the period after the Babylonian exile, when Aramaic began to be spoken by the Israelites.

3. "The Words of the Wise" (22:17–24:22) contain both proverbs and instructions. They are an Israelite adaptation of the Egyptian "Sayings of Amenemope," a pharaoh of the tenth century BC. These were translated into Hebrew and transformed by Israelite faith and morals. This fact requires dating these verses after Amenemope became pharaoh, which places them during the lifetime of Solomon. The Hebrew form of these sayings may be Solomonic or from even later in the monarchic era.

4. "These Are Also the Sayings of the Wise" (24:23–34) is a title that refers to five undatable sayings against laziness and partiality in judging legal cases.

5. "The Proverbs of Solomon Which the Men of Hezekiah King of Judah Copied" (25–29) includes two sections: chapters 25–27, mainly synthetic proverbs, and chapters 28–29, mostly antithetic proverbs. This collection may date to the reign of Hezekiah (715–689 BC).

6. "The Words of Agur, Son of Jaqeh" (30) are mostly undatable numerical proverbs about the mysterious God.

7. "The Words of Lemuel, King of Massa" (31:1–9) warn a prince against women, wine, and injustice to the poor. There are no clues for dating this collection since Lemuel is otherwise unknown.
8. Finally, 31:10–31 is an undatable alphabetic acrostic praising the perfect wife. The acrostic device begins each line of the poem with a successive letter of the Hebrew aleph-beth (Hebrew for "alphabet"). This device cannot be translated into other languages.

This book on Proverbs will examine various themes found throughout the book, since there is no thematic organization within the text itself. Although there are many fine commentaries on the Proverbs that examine each proverb in the order found in the text, it seemed more helpful to many readers to take the book thematically. We hope this helps you understand wisdom more deeply and motivates you to use the Proverbs more often in your daily life.

PART 1

Family

CHAPTER 1

Husbands and Wives

The book of Proverbs offers husbands and wives timeless common sense for both the good and bad times of marriage. As the authors of Proverbs understand, only by recognizing the positive characteristics of marriage as well as its greatest challenges can you truly grasp its real value.

A continual dripping on a rainy day and a contentious woman are alike. (Prov. 27:15)

Now, we should begin by saying that these references to women and wives apply just as much to men and husbands. The writers of Proverbs were men, and so the sayings on marriage often single out women, but we know that men can be just as querulous and contentious as women—although sometimes in different ways. Men, you aren't off the hook!

Why do the writers of the Proverbs compare constant nagging and nitpicking to "dripping on a rainy day"? Picture an ancient Israelite house, which had a roof made of flimsy boards topped with packed soil and straw. When it rained, the water would eventually go through the straw, pick up some mud and dirt, and drip through the cracks between the boards of the ceiling. You can just imagine how annoying and frustrating (and messy) that would be.

This constant, noisy, muddy drip is what unresolved quarreling is like. Once it gets started, it is difficult to figure out how to stop it quickly, and so it becomes a source of annoyance and even anger—enough to drive anyone crazy. Like a drip you can't escape, constant nagging and unresolved tensions in marriage make everything—even the good times—difficult to enjoy.

And what is it that prevents this dripping? The only way for an ancient Israelite to keep it under control was to ensure that his home was constantly maintained. He'd have to take care of the roof by changing the straw, replenishing the soil, and keeping the boards in good shape.

By analogy, the way a husband and a wife can avoid that continuous nagging—that nit-nit-nitpicking—is to keep their relationship in constant repair. A couple can't avoid this relationship maintenance because eventually it will rain. There will be bills to be paid, stress from overwork, health issues, problems with raising the children, and so on. If a couple is not ready when the problems and challenges pour like cats and dogs, that annoying drip-drip-drip will drive them mad until they end up fighting like cats and dogs.

Communication between a husband and wife is one of the most important maintenance issues in any marriage. They need always to pay close attention to their lines of communication. And what makes the difference between quarrelsome argumentation and healthy communication? The first step is to communicate honestly, but without judgment. This doesn't mean that you don't point out things that are causing difficulty in your relationship. That kind of avoidance just allows things to get worse. Rather, you must communicate in a way that *informs* the other of a difficulty—something that he or she probably didn't even recognize—without *blaming*. Blame and judgment lead, naturally, to defensiveness, and then to hard-heartedness.

Maintenance of a relationship is a two-person job; you and your spouse have to be in it together. Both avoiding those repairs and arguing based on blame and judgment will allow the drips to continue—and to get worse. And the longer that annoying drip, drip, drip goes on, the harder it will be to fight through it to complete the hard work of repairing the roof—or your marriage.

A good wife is the crown of her husband. (Prov. 12:4)

In the Maronite Rite and other eastern rites of the Catholic Church, it is still the custom to crown the bride and groom during the wedding ceremony. This beautiful ceremony not only brings to mind the beauty of the teaching of this proverb but also reminds us that while this aphorism is gender-specific, it applies to men and women, both of whom can learn from it.

How do you relate to your wife or to your husband? Is your spouse like a crown on your head? A crown accents beauty by drawing attention to the face through its beautiful ornamentation. A crown holds a place of honor on the person wearing it, sitting upon the head so that all can see its beauty. This applies nicely to one's spouse. The more you see and appreciate the treasury of goodness in your spouse's mind, heart, soul, and actions, the more your spouse accents your own goodness. It is through honoring one another that the beauty of each person grows, enhancing the other person at the same time.

Things that are the same do not accent, highlight, or draw attention to one another; rather, they wash each other out with their sameness. Similarly, the differences between a man and a woman allow each to crown the other by their complementary distinctiveness. A husband delights in the differences between himself and his wife, even when he doesn't fully understand them. A wife grows to appreciate what makes her husband distinct from her by honoring and respecting him. In so doing, each accents the other's best qualities.

Spouses become better within themselves by seeking out ways to show honor to the other—not to control, to dominate, or to compete. Life is not a contest or a competition—and marriage certainly is not. It is in mutual respect that we find lasting peace and joy.

A gracious woman gets honor, and violent men get riches. (Prov. 11:16)

At first glance, it might seem that this proverb is saying that women are ordered to graciousness and men to violence, but this isn't the case at all. A strong, aggressive man might be able to get wealth and possessions, but the writer is not holding that quality up for praise. Rather, he is setting up an antithesis between the godly honor of the gracious woman and the worldly riches of the violent man.

This proverb is also an observation of the timeless fact that men tend to identify themselves with what they can accomplish and accumulate. It's so easy for us—men and women alike—to find our identities not in the Lord and His Church, but in our houses, cars, bank accounts, and other possessions. Not only does this proverb set that attitude against the personal quality of graciousness that leads to true honor, but it associates acquisition with violence. This is strong medicine.

On the other hand, the woman who is gracious from her very heart in her relationships with others—that is, the woman who is kind, gentle, and loving—is honored by God and man. But this applies just as much to men, who are also honored for their kindness and compassion—especially when that graciousness comes from the prudent use of their physical strength.

Truly gracious and virtuous men and women avoid using physical strength, or any other powerful quality, such as mental agility, magnetic charisma, or business acumen, in a way that controls others—that turns them into instruments for the acquisition of wealth, power, and other forms of self-aggrandizement. This is a kind of violence.

Rather, all of these powers and talents are gifts from God. Because they are gifts He has graciously poured upon us, we must consider what God wants us to do with them. How can I share with my family the gifts God has freely and undeservedly granted me? How does He want me to use them to help the poor or the needy? When we use our gifts as God wishes, graciousness circumvents violent, selfish usage, and we become better for it.

He who finds a wife finds a good thing. (Prov. 18:22)

In another translation, this proverb says more straightforwardly that a good wife (or husband!) is "a good in itself." That is, it is inherently good to find a good spouse; a spouse is, to paraphrase the second part of the saying, a favor bestowed by God. There's a related proverb that gets at this same point: "House and wealth are inherited from fathers, but a prudent wife is from the LORD" (Prov. 19:14).

God did not establish marriage as a situation into which two people simply fall. Neither is marriage just some job or a task that you perform; it's a vocation. What does *vocation* mean? The word comes from the Latin *vocare*, "to call," indicating that a vocation is a calling from God. He calls a man and a woman to matrimony because this is the state of life in which He wants a particular couple to live out their way to Heaven and away from Hell; He calls you to your spouse.

We have to be careful not to equate the feeling of love or attraction with the vocation to marriage. There might be many people to whom you could be attracted — many people with whom you have that sensation of "love at first sight." And why is that? Often this happens because someone reminds us of the first man or woman we loved — our father or mother. We recognize some idealized quality of our parents in another person, and we fall in love with that ideal. That's normal, and we should expect it. After all, one of the main points of parenting is to model what proper love looks like.

But that immediate infatuation is not enough. Every man and woman needs to take time alone with the Lord to pray and consider that marriage is a vocation to which God calls him or her. In prayer, ask yourself: How will I make God, who gave me (or will give me) this other person as a spouse, the center of my marriage? The way to find the love that God has in store for you in matrimony, as well as to sustain it through every day of your married life, is to cultivate a deeper and closer relationship with Jesus Christ.

A tremendous irony of love shows itself when your relationship with God is the center of your life and your marriage: with God at the center, you will love your spouse far more than if you had put him or her on the pedestal reserved for God alone. Why is that? Quite simply and logically, whenever we put a fellow human being ahead of God, we inevitably expect that person to be as good as God. No human person or institution is capable of being as good, wise, or powerful as God, and a person will inevitably disappoint and infuriate when he or she fails to meet those standards.

However, when God is the center of a family, each member becomes free to accept the others as merely fellow human sinners, each with his or her own faults. When God is the Lord of the family, He forgives each family member of their sins and frees everyone to forgive each other's faults and failings as well.

Never forget that your spouse is a gift from the Lord. Treasure him or her as you would treasure any gift from such an extraordinary Giver, and show Him your gratitude by remaining close to Him always.

CHAPTER 2

Parents and Children

The ancient Israelites had crying babies, ornery toddlers, difficult preteens, and rebellious adolescents, just as we do. Raising good children is essential to the well-being of any society. And since raising children is an important part of daily life, the book of Proverbs has a great deal to say about it.

These proverbs focus on the duties that parents and children owe to each other — especially when it comes to discipline. The family is the first place where we learn and practice the mutual responsibilities that make society possible. More than that, though, the family is the first place where we learn and practice the virtues that help us, with God's grace, to grow in holiness. Proverbs looks to parents as the great teachers of children, so we seek wisdom in this area of family life, too.

Folly is bound up in the heart of a child, but the rod of discipline drives it far from him. (Prov. 22:15)

First of all, while what we today call spanking was the norm in ancient Israel, we should read references to "the rod" to refer to firm discipline generally, not just physical punishment. You don't have to have a particular position on spanking to take wisdom from these proverbs.

There are two types of "folly" that need to be removed from children by their parents' discipline: intellectual and moral. The first is a little bit easier to handle, but we shouldn't overlook it.

Quite simply, children need to be taught about the world. They need to understand what's dangerous, what's helpful, what words mean (and what words not to say!), and so on.

Often this kind of teaching just happens over the course of daily life. But it also requires a certain discipline. Remember that parents are naturally the first and primary educators of their children. This discipline might include more structured approaches, such as scheduled story times or inviting the children to learn daily life skills that are appropriate to their age level—cleaning, cooking, repairing, and so on. It will also entail parental vigilance to correct the little ones when they "goof up" through inattention or by mischievous malice. Ultimately, it's up to parents to provide the basic common sense about the world that allows kids to become more independent over time.

Then there's moral folly. This reminds us of St. Augustine's words about young children: that they have all the inclination to sin that adults have, but lack only the strength to carry it out. It's up to parents, then, to channel children's energies toward goodness and virtue. Otherwise, young people often develop habits of vice that become much more difficult to break later on.

I've always found this illustration, which I learned from a psychologist, to be very helpful. There's a type of training called isometric exercise, in which someone pushes against an immovable object, such as a door frame, in order to strengthen muscles. By analogy, children need moral isometric exercise. Inevitably they will push against their parents to try to get their way. Parents, on the other hand, must be like the door frame: immovable objects against which children will strengthen their moral muscles by pushing hard but losing to the strength of Mom and Dad, united in virtue, moral instruction, and discipline.

Being a firm, virtuous door frame is not always an easy or glamorous job. Parents might take a little abuse now and again—yelling and pouting and so on (for which clear and definite discipline might need to be applied). Yet without the parents' moral strength standing up to the child's willfulness, those moral muscles will never develop. Isometrics don't work when a child pushes against a rocking chair!

Every child is born with a different personality, so each one has different needs in regard to learning and discipline. Parents are commonly amazed at the differences in character and personality of each infant, even among twins, a phenomenon I have observed in my nieces and nephews and other children—their personalities are distinct and unique at such young ages! An important component of parenting is prayerful consideration of each child's personality, character, and specific needs in order for parents to "drive out" the "folly" of youth and inexperience.

He who spares the rod hates his son, but he who loves him is diligent to discipline him. (Prov. 13:24)

As with the last proverb we looked at, this one doesn't mean that you have to strike your children physically to be a good parent. It does mean that discipline—firm discipline—is an essential part of true love.

One of the biggest difficulties I see in counseling parents is when they let little transgressions continue and repeat until they become big problems. Finally, at one point, parents blow up in anger, provoked to "losing their temper," rather than using controlled anger and loving correction. At the point when parents "lose their temper," they have let the emotion of anger take control, and their acts of discipline are more directed toward expressing their frustration with the child rather than toward teaching and correcting the child. Children can detect this shift of attention, even if they do not know how to put it into words, and their hearts can become hardened to the point at which they yell back, "I hate you, Mommy and Daddy." They rarely actually hate their parents at that point, but they are using the strongest words they know to express their own anger, justified or not, at their parents. Such actions by children and parents can cause their relationship to deteriorate to the point that real discipline becomes impossible.

This is where the proverb's concern for "diligence" comes into play. Good discipline cannot be an on-again, off-again part of family life; parents exercise constant diligence so that bad habits do not become entrenched in children. We shouldn't kid ourselves: this is hard work! And it's hard work not only physically but also emotionally. We always want people we love to be happy at all times, but diligent discipline often means upsetting children who insist on doing their own thing at their own convenience for their own (often selfish) reasons. It may hurt to say no when an adorable child desperately wants something. But that child won't be so adorable in a few years if he never experiences proper correction that guides and directs him away from self-centered and even egomaniacal tyranny to a more polite, thoughtful, and sharing disposition.

Good discipline, however, does not mean that parents are supposed to harangue their children to the point of despair. If discipline is too constant and too harsh, it becomes easy for kids to feel as if they'll never be good enough—and they just give up. Parents need not constantly *look for* things to get upset about. Diligence does not mean obsession.

I'll never forget, when I was about six years old, when my three year-old brother said a racial slur in front of my mother. He had no idea what it meant, but words like that were unfortunately too common in south Florida in the 1950s, so he picked it up somewhere. (This is a good reminder: even young toddlers are listening and learning to everything they hear around them!) And even though my brother was barely more than a toddler, my mother turned around, gave him a tap on the mouth, and said firmly, "Don't you ever say that again." And I said, sensing the seriousness, "None of us will ever say that." And we didn't. She never let the idea that racist words were acceptable get a foothold in our family—even at a very young age. This principle applies to every other form of immorality: parents can and should nip it in the bud before it becomes a habit.

He who does violence to his father and chases away his mother
is a son who causes shame and brings reproach. (Prov. 19:26)

This proverb shifts the focus from parents' responsibilities to children's responsibilities. Let's focus especially on the second part of this saying, which has become more relevant than ever.

Modern people are living longer (in the 1890s, life expectancy was forty-five; in the twenty-first century, it is close to eighty); therefore, our responsibilities to older family members have increased. Naturally, people are making a lot of money out of this reality: "Elder care" is now a massive and profitable industry. In many cases, professional care of the elderly is truly essential, as with illnesses such as Alzheimer's disease. There are also plenty of situations, however, when family members practically "chase away" their older relatives so as to avoid their needs, their repetitive stories, and other inconveniences. The culture is struggling to deal with our special responsibilities to our elderly parents and grandparents, and all too often the elderly suffer neglect or lonely abandonment.

This proverb warns that intentionally ignoring our parents' needs brings "shame and . . . reproach." This is true for two reasons. First, most obviously, our parents sacrificed so much for us. They changed diapers, cleaned vomit, and disciplined us even when it was hard or inconvenient. When my mother had late-stage cancer, she wanted to stay at home, where she was comfortable, so my siblings and I took care of her. We did for her all the things she did for us for so many years: we helped her to communicate, helped her to the bathroom at night, and so on. As my brother Jimmy and I carried her to that bathroom in the middle of the night, I told her, "Mom, you always said that paybacks are hell. You walked the floor with us in the middle of the night, and now we get to do it for you." The very least that we children can do is take care of our aged and ailing parents: love them and nourish them so that when they go to meet Christ, they are surrounded by our love. In fact, standing by Mom's bed until she breathed her last remains one of the most privileged moments of my life.

Secondly, caring for our aging parents is so important because it shows the world that the infirm are not inconveniences to be "chased away." We have a duty to care for our parents, not just as a kind of payback for their "labors of love" in raising us. It is a Christian duty to care for the elderly, the sick, the infirm, and the weak. Family life shouldn't be the limit of our charity; it should be a training ground for wider charity that extends beyond the family to other needy people.

———————— ❀ ————————

Train up a child in the way he should go, and when he is old he will not depart from it. (Prov. 22:6)

This proverb is a reassuring promise — and at the same time a reminder of parents' huge responsibility. The lessons parents teach young children stay with them for the rest of their lives. We can all, I'm sure, trace many of our character traits to our upbringing.

Of course, this doesn't mean that children's fates are sealed by their first several years. Parents can seemingly do everything perfectly, but when free will kicks into an adolescent's life, children can go off the rails because they choose to do so. However, it remains true that those earliest childhood lessons in goodness and love are never fully erased; they can serve as a sturdy anchor to which prodigal children can grab hold and return to the path of virtue and holiness. The work parents do to form their children is never in vain, despite appearances to the contrary.

Parents, do not forget that God's grace is always working in the life of every single person, including errant children. God our Lord loves your children infinitely more than you do and eternally longer than you do. Never cease praying for your children—neither when times are good, nor, especially, when times are bad. Jesus Christ is always there to heal wounds, forgive bad behavior, and redirect sinners toward goodness.

CHAPTER 3

Wisdom and Chastity

We often think about living the virtue of chastity—that is, abstinence before marriage and fidelity within marriage—as little more than a question of willpower. But as with any virtue, if we just rely on our own wills, we'll certainly fall at some point. The book of Proverbs, on the other hand, connects the virtue of chastity with the gift of wisdom. We'll consider the connection between the two in this chapter.

The fear of the Lord is the beginning of knowledge; fools despise wisdom and instruction. (Prov. 1:7)

Many people misunderstand the concept of "fear of the Lord." It sounds like a dark emotion, apparently setting up God as an adversary to His people. It is just the opposite, however. The fear of the Lord is not the fear of something terrible and frightening, but a fear that is rooted in love and flows from it, such as a child's fear of disappointing a parent.

We fear the Lord not because He is out to get us, but because He has the power to do anything He wills, and yet He chooses to love us and nurture us with His grace. That power should be awe-inspiring. And His awesome graciousness toward us small human beings should evoke in us an awesome feeling of gratitude—as well as an awesome fear of doing anything that would offend such a wonderful God.

Not to have that fear is to take for granted all that God does for us. That would imply a kind of presumption that no matter what we do, the Lord will be okay with it. Such an idea would lead us astray, because we would eventually rely on our own selfish standard of conduct rather than the Lord's standards for the greater good of ourselves, our neighbors, and our world.

Wisdom and knowledge begin with fear of the Lord because without an appreciation and respect for His infinite and eternal power, we will not appreciate and respect His infinite and eternal truth. We easily become arrogant about our opinions and plans, failing to consider the effects they might have beyond our self-centered desires. We end up relying on ourselves and on the surrounding culture for wisdom, rather than seeking the deeper wisdom of God's truth. The next proverbs discuss the dangers of that type of arrogant thinking.

Because they hated knowledge and did not choose the fear of the Lord, would have none of my counsel, and despised all my reproof, therefore they shall eat the fruit of their way and be sated with their own devices. For waywardness kills the simple, and the complacency of fools destroys them; but those who listen to me will be secure and will live at ease, without dread of disaster. (Prov. 1:29–33)

At this point in the book of Proverbs, these words are placed in the mouth of Wisdom personified. Israel's wisdom literature frequently personifies Wisdom as a lady, both because the Hebrew word for *wisdom* is a feminine noun and because it is usually pretty easy to get male adolescent students to think about and listen to a beautiful woman.

The writer of these verses connects the fool's rejection of fear of the Lord with his rejection of wisdom. What results from the double rejection? The individuals who rely only upon themselves become fools, "sated with their own devices." In other words, they become satisfied with their own disordered desires, rather than with the wisdom that comes from the Lord.

Let's focus on this line: "The complacency of fools destroys them." Foolish people are often full of self-confidence. Part of the problem in recent decades is that our society has placed such a premium on self-confidence—and not being shy about it—that it is taught in school as a primary virtue. After the Supreme Court made it illegal to teach religion in government-run schools (in 1962 in *Engel v. Vitale*), these schools gave up the metaphysical and religious basis for moral teaching. As a result, the highest value promoted by the state has been absolute freedom rather than God's commandments or virtue.

Without some notion of God, how can a person come to an understanding of the meaning of what is good? How would government-run schools determine virtue and distinguish it from vice? Without God's commandments and the fear of breaking them, what would motivate a person to be virtuous, except that a teacher might recommend it? Therefore, in place of virtue, the schools recommend self-confidence and positive self-image.

However, as often as not, experience indicates that self-confidence is merely a mask for ignorance and bluster. Too often we meet people who impress themselves and others with their self-confidence but who have neither the knowledge nor the wisdom to back it up. The literature on narcissists and sociopaths commonly indicate a high, toxic level of self-confidence that makes the sociopath capable of trampling on anyone around him in order to acquire what he believes he deserves.

Complacency and self-confidence are frequently two sides of the same coin. People who place their faith in themselves soon think they are perfect and no longer have to work to be better, to grow in virtue, to avoid sin, and so on. That is the point when the evil spirit likes to strike. Right when people think they have gotten everything figured out for themselves without the wisdom of the Lord, that is when they are most vulnerable to temptation, particularly sexual temptation.

Then you will understand righteousness and justice and equity, every good path; for wisdom will come into your heart, and knowledge will be pleasant to your soul; prudence will watch over you; and understanding will guard you. . . . You will be saved from the loose woman, from the adulteress with her smooth words. (Prov. 2:9–11, 16)

This passage explains some of the benefits of having a healthy fear of the Lord and seeking out His wisdom. It finishes with a reference to the "loose woman" and the "adulteress," but, of course, these terms could refer to either men or women who choose to embrace sexual immorality. The book of Proverbs was probably written for young men pursuing civil-service work in the royal court or as ambassadors, so the warnings to the young men are concerned with the opposite sex. However, men with bad intentions are just as likely to try to woo with "smooth words" as are women, so this saying applies equally to men.

The idea in the first clause that wisdom will allow us to "understand righteousness" is so important. It's one thing merely to *know* what is right and to do it out of obedience. There's nothing wrong with that, especially at the beginning stages of becoming morally alert. It is better, however, to *understand* the wisdom about moral goodness and then live it out because we believe it is for our good. Furthermore, when we understand the reasons and inherent goodness of God's moral law, we become better evangelists who are more prepared both to resist temptation when it presents itself and to explain the good sense of the moral teaching to others. The capacity for understanding the wisdom of God's morality is even more important in the modern age, when so many people are relativists who deny that there is an objective moral law or even objective truth.

We see a similar concept in the phrase "knowledge will be pleasant to your soul." When we have a relationship with Christ and pursue His truth, we do not mope around complaining and whining about doing the right thing—we enjoy goodness simply because it is good in itself! True knowledge feels welcome in our souls, and good actions and decisions come more naturally. Even when choosing to do the right thing becomes more challenging and difficult, the good habits will "watch over" and "guard" us from being comfortable with evil decisions. We learn to prefer the good for its own sake.

According to the last part of this passage, wisdom will protect us against those who would tempt us to sexual immorality. Now, this translation uses the phrase "loose woman," but other translations say "strange woman." This is an important word choice. Remember: no word in Sacred Scripture is without meaning.

Even in ancient Israel it was known that people would be more likely to seek out illicit sexual encounters with people they didn't know. Today we talk about the "hookup culture" and "one-night stands," but this is hardly a new phenomenon. In my experience counseling people who have struggled with sexual sin, they describe the appeal of an anonymous tryst: no relationship, no responsibility, no emotional connection, and, we like to think, no guilt. We want to use someone and then discard him or her. It's the "throwaway culture," Pope Francis has decried.

Of course, in practice it never quite works that way. There's no way to be so intimate with another person without forming some connection. And there's always the guilt that comes with having violated God's law. That pain lasts, and I see it all the time in counseling. And it is wisdom—and the prudence and understanding that come with it—that gives us the spiritual and psychological resources to be able to say no when the "smooth" tempter comes along.

And now, my child, listen to me, and do not depart from the words of my mouth. Keep your way far from her, and do not go near the door of her house. (Prov. 5:7–8)

These verses, which are part of an instruction on the loose woman versus the good wife (Prov. 5:1–23), offer an important component of understanding sexual morality. The "her" in this verse refers to the "loose" or "strange" woman. The counsel is not just to choose not to give in to temptation but to *avoid* it entirely. Today we call this avoiding "the near occasions of sin."

One of the most common mistakes we make with regard to temptation of any kind, but especially sexual temptation, is to linger around it, assuming we can "handle it" and resist giving in. We all too frequently put ourselves in situations—at bars, or alone in dorms or apartments, or with sexually explicit media—in which we know temptation will occur, foolishly thinking that we have the self-control to go just so far without going too far. However, this is the "complacency of fools" we discussed in a previous proverb. It is self-confidence without wisdom, and it typically leads to ruin when the passions take over. All the self-confidence in the world does not matter when a person gives over control of his will to the emotional and physical reactions to sexual arousal.

A great fruit of wisdom with regard to sexuality is understanding oneself enough to know when temptation is near, followed by the ability to summon the strength and self-control to get out of the situation before it's too late. When married people talk about their sexual sin, they rarely say that they went out one day looking to commit adultery with a stranger. Rather, things started up seemingly innocently: a private conversation, then a coffee date, then a little peck on the cheek, and so on. And when things finally went way too far, people always say, "I never meant for it to get to this point." And I'm sure they didn't! But they never did anything to stop it either. That's how occasions of sin get us.

It takes the wisdom that comes from a relationship with the Lord to be able to resist not just sexual sin itself but the occasions of sin that might seem fun and innocent at first. No fun is worth risking mortal sin over. Let us resolve to appeal to the Lord in prayer when temptation strikes, so that we may know when to get out of danger before it's too late.

Once a lady in my television audience asked me if I ever learned any spiritual lessons while I was hunting. I told her about a hunt when I tied a string on a cotton ball, dipped it in doe's estrous scent, tied it to my boot and walked along a deer path. I untied the string, hung it in a tree, and climbed into my deer stand to wait for dawn. An eleven-point old buck came up on the path, his nose to the ground following that scent right into the sight of my rifle. The lesson is this: Sex makes you stupid, and then you die. I have not met a man yet who disagrees with me.

CHAPTER 4

Tenderness and Toughness

Love in any context, but especially in a family, will alternate between tenderness and toughness. The ancient Israelites recognized that love does not look like the saccharine romances (they were blessed not to know about artificial sugar) that are sold in pop culture. Love is not merely a feeling that comes and goes, making us feel warm and cuddly when it's here and cold and prickly when it's gone. Love is a choice that includes wisdom, prudence, and the hard work of self-giving.

Every proverb in this chapter includes the phrase "loyalty and faithfulness," which is a translation of the Hebrew word *hesed*, a term referring specifically to "covenant love." This is an important concept to understand before meditating on the individual proverbs.

Among the ancient Israelites and their neighbors, a covenant was not merely a contract for various services rendered, although covenants did include some specific stipulations. Rather, a covenant established a relationship between the covenant partners, as well as a lifelong promise to accept that relationship and to fulfill certain responsibilities to the other members of the covenant. These agreements might be between nations, individuals, or clans, but the most famous covenants in the Bible were between God and His people, Israel. For instance, God made a covenant with Abraham after he demonstrated his willingness to give everything back to God, even if it meant sacrificing his son Isaac:

> And the angel of the LORD called to Abraham a second time
> from heaven, and said, "By myself I have sworn, says the

LORD, because you have done this, and have not withheld your son, your only son, I will indeed bless you, and I will multiply your descendants as the stars of heaven and as the sand which is on the seashore." (Gen. 22:15–17)

With the angel's statement, God announces His irrevocable commitment to Abraham and His descendants. Now, these commitments might just sound like fancy versions of what we would call contracts, but that wouldn't be right. A contract is a simple agreement to provide certain goods or services, such as when a person hires a cook or a gardener. A covenant is more like a marriage, in which one's very identity is changed through establishing a new relationship with a spouse in an irreversible lifelong relationship that includes God as the enforcer of the commitment. Even when God isn't making the covenant, the individuals or families who are party to the covenant swear before God—not just a lawyer or a magistrate—that they will fulfill the commitment they're making.

Hesed, or "covenant love," then, is the love proper to a committed, covenantal relationship: total, self-giving, self-sacrificing, never ending, and based in the love of God. Such love may change its appearance over time—sometimes passionate, sometimes staid; sometimes tender, sometimes tough—but it never changes in the depth of commitment to the other person. That's what these proverbs mean by "loyalty and faithfulness": unconditional love.

Let not loyalty and faithfulness forsake you; bind them about your neck, write them on the tablet of your heart. (Prov. 3:3)

This proverb urges us to make covenant love the center of our lives by giving us images of a necklace and "the tablet of your heart."

The necklace reminds us that unconditional love should always be with us. As Catholics, we make this reminder tangible to ourselves and others by wearing a crucifix necklace or the scapular of Our Lady of Mount Carmel. Some translations read that we keep *hesed* "around [our] throat." This image suggests that covenant love is as essential to life as the air, drink, and food that pass through our throats.

The next image brings to mind several other moments in the Bible. Soon after the Babylonians had destroyed Jerusalem (587 BC), the Lord spoke to the prophet Jeremiah of the new covenant, which Jesus Christ would fulfill: "I will put my law within them, and I will write it upon their hearts; and I will be their God, and they shall be my people" (Jer. 31:33). At the Last Supper, Jesus instituted the Eucharist as His Blood of the "new and everlasting covenant"; this covenant is rooted in the Blood of Jesus Christ, as the New Testament makes clear numerous times.

Then, St. Paul writes that when the Gentiles "do by nature what the law requires ... even though they do not have the law ... they show that what the law requires is written on their hearts" (Rom. 2:14–15). He also speaks of his own belief in this way: "For I delight in the law of God, in my inmost self" (Rom. 7:22). In fact, the concept of the law resting in the hearts of men is a running theme in St. Paul's letters:

> You yourselves are our letter of recommendation, written on your hearts, to be known and read by all men; and you show that you are a letter from Christ delivered by us, written not with ink but with the Spirit of the living God, not on tablets of stone but on tablets of human hearts. (2 Cor. 3:2–3)

> This is the covenant that I will make with them after those days, says the Lord: I will put my laws on their hearts, and write them on their minds. (Heb. 10:16)

> This is the covenant that I will make with the house of
> Israel after those days, says the Lord: I will put my laws into
> their minds, and write them on their hearts, and I will be
> their God, and they shall be my people. (Heb. 8:10)

The Lord writes His covenant and His laws in our hearts, including and especially the law that we live by covenant love. Clearly, the Lord does not want us to live by merely obeying laws and living out the covenant relationship through mere external observance. Rather, His desire is to effect a transformation of every human heart so that the covenantal love of God—and the necessary inclusion of the neighbor in that love—flows from the depths of the human heart.

Jesus so obviously desired this kind of transformation of the heart that when He taught about the commandments of God in the Sermon on the Mount, he *expanded* on their meaning and application (see Matt. 5:20–48). "Thou shalt not kill" requires more than simply avoiding murder; it requires a transformed heart that does not call one's enemy a fool or try to get revenge. "Thou shalt not commit adultery" comes to include refusing even to look upon others with lust. "Thou shalt not swear a false oath" becomes a prohibition against all oaths because one must always tell the truth. Clearly, God desires that covenant love and its specific behavior should flow from the heart.

> *Do they not err that devise evil? Those who devise good meet
> loyalty and faithfulness. (Prov. 14:22)*

The Hebrew word for "those who devise evil" is *chorshei*, which refers to plowing fields in an erratic manner. So, those who devise evil follow their own paths in which they chase their own (usually selfish) desires instead of following the straight path of virtue that the Lord has set out for them. The result is a poor harvest, whether of vegetables or of holiness.

On the other hand, those who plow the fields in straight lines, that is, those who follow the Lord's paths of righteousness and goodness, will encounter covenant love and faithfulness. The link between following God's law and living in the light of unconditional love is important, particularly in a contemporary culture that denies and rejects that link. For instance, people often set up a false choice between love and following the rules, as in the song lyric, "If loving you is wrong, then I don't want to be right." Many people think that loving others entails accepting almost anything they might desire or do—and that loving themselves means indulging every desire that comes along.

This proverb presents an opposing position: following God's law leads us to authentic love and personal freedom. If you speak to someone who has used his or her freedom to abuse drugs and alcohol or to use pornography or to pursue serial sexual relationships, you won't hear a story of liberation but one of slavery to the addictiveness of sin.

In reality, we humans cannot fully and freely give unconditional love without following God's law, and we cannot fully follow God's law without unconditional love. When a child, a family member, or a friend goes astray (*chorshei*), true love summons us correct him or her, whether gently or with toughness. People who fall into sin hurt themselves and usually the people around them. Love does not let them continue to harm themselves—and worse, it does not affirm them in bad decisions. Accepting their destructive sinful behavior might seem easier at first, but it is not the authentic good that we desire for the person we claim to love.

Another aspect of fulfilling our duties to God and living covenant love belongs to our work, whether inside or outside the home. When we labor for our own glory rather than for the glory of God and the needs of our family and neighbors, we are not practicing covenant love. It's easy to think that success in our jobs—getting awards, promotions, and so on—means that we are following God's path. But if we are pursuing those honors to stoke our egos rather than for the sake of others, covenant love is not the operating dynamic in our lives and we are not "devising good." Moral goodness and self-giving love belong together, and we mature by integrating them in every aspect of our lives—Church, family, friends, society, work, play, and so on.

By loyalty and faithfulness iniquity is atoned for, and by the fear of the LORD a man avoids evil. (Prov. 16:6)

When people live in close quarters, whether in a family or, as I did, in religious community with other priests and seminarians, they learn to deal with each other's rough edges. We all have them, even if we don't realize it. The first part of this proverb tells us how true covenant love helps us to cope with the difficult aspects of others' personalities, as well as our own.

When the wisdom writer says that by covenant love "iniquity is atoned for," he does not mean that our love magically wipes away sins. For that, we need God's grace, which is granted by Jesus Christ's saving death on the Cross, especially as ministered in the sacrament of Confession. This proverb teaches that unconditional love makes wrongs easier to bear and can help others to overcome their struggles.

The assurance that we are acting in love makes all the difference. When I lived in community with my brother Jesuits, they often had to call me out when I was having trouble fulfilling my duties to the community. I frequently tried to take on too many activities at once, and it took the loving correction of those around me to get me to focus on my primary responsibilities. The key to accepting their correction is that I always knew, based on the way they treated me in everyday life—with kindness and prayer and support—that this correction was based on love, not malice. Their love helped me correct my faults.

It's the same in any family. It is so important that parents tell children that they love them, and there is no such thing as too much love. Of course, when the time comes for toughness, they are assured (even though it might not always seem like it to children at the moment) that correction is coming from their parents' unconditional love, not from rejection, contempt, or pride. When they know they are loved and that their parents are helping them become better persons through discipline, they will accept that discipline sooner than parents expect. As children discover and work through their unique pains and struggles, the covenant love of parents helps them smooth out their rough edges and forms them into wonderful young women and men.

The second part of this proverb reminds us that our acts of covenant love always are better when they are done in union with love and fear of the Lord. Left to ourselves, human love is tinged with pride and self-regard, but our Lord enables us to practice authentic unconditional love. Our love for others becomes a reflection of His love for us; whereas, when we detach ourselves from His love, our own love for others suffers in turn.

Remember that Jesus said that "the great and first commandment" is "You shall love the Lord your God with all your heart, and with all your soul, and with all your mind" (Matt. 22:37, 38). Love Him with everything you have—all of which He has given you anyway. When you love God first, you love His creatures even better. If you love God above everything else, then, you won't expect your spouse and children to be God; that is, you can let them be the fallible people they are—just like you. His love makes it possible to bring people away from the path of evil.

PART 2

Justice

CHAPTER 5

Leadership and Righteousness

Scholars generally agree, based on evidence in the text, that the sages who wrote and compiled the book of Proverbs included retired politicians and statesmen — ambassadors, civil servants, and other public figures. These government officials often had kings, governments, and politics on their minds, and so concerns related to public policy and administration run through the book. For instance, chapter 20 has a number of proverbs about the relationship to the king; the "Sayings of the Wise" (22:17—24:22) offer admonitions to be humble to urban, upper-class youths who will face the responsibilities and temptations of their status; and the section entitled "Further Sayings of the Wise" (24:23–34) criticizes laziness and partiality in judging legal cases. Other proverbs scattered throughout the book also deal with political and judicial issues so as to give young men wisdom for life in the royal court and in the judicial system.

Of course, Proverbs assumes that the government is a monarchy, as was the case in Israel and Judah. Like most other monarchs in the ancient world, the kings of Israel and Judah had nearly total authority, living wealthy lifestyles superior to and apart from the ordinary lives of the people they ruled. Yet, unlike the majority of neighboring ancient monarchs, the kings of Israel were bound by God's law like every ordinary Israelite. The Old Testament contains many episodes about prophets "speaking truth to power" by confronting kings of Israel for their misdeeds. These range from David's adultery with Bathsheba and murder of her husband (2 Samuel 11), to Ahab's murder of Naboth and confiscation of his vineyard (1 Kings 21)—plus idolatry, corruption, and other violations of God's commandments.

We can see here the beginnings of the new idea of the equality of every person, whether commoner or high born, before God and His Law, which informed Christian politics for centuries. The Proverbs give a kind of wisdom that warns students against presumption before powerful kings and warns kings about presumption before the Lord God. The following proverbs are not simply insights into ancient political practices; they have great relevance for our own day, as well. While times change, some principles, even in politics and judicial practice, are timeless.

* * *

I have good advice and sound wisdom; I have insight, I have strength. By me kings reign, and rulers decree what is just; by me rulers rule, and nobles, all who govern rightly. (Prov. 8:14–16)

These words are part of a long instruction in which the personified Lady Wisdom speaks about her benefits and background (Prov. 8:1–36). The Hebrew word for "wisdom" is feminine, so it is portrayed not as an abstraction but as a person, "Lady Wisdom," who summons all people, including the fools and simpletons, to learn from her. The verses cited here summon kings and good rulers to seek wisdom's guidance, which can be seen as the sages' extension to every ruler of Isaiah's prophecy for the Messiah: "The spirit of the LORD shall rest on him, the spirit of wisdom and understanding, the spirit of counsel and might, the spirit of knowledge and the fear of the LORD" (Isa. 11:2). Kings need to rule with the guidance of the gifts of the Spirit, especially wisdom.

In modern democratic societies, the power rests, at least in theory, with the people—the voters who select representatives and executives. These democracies rejected their earlier monarchic governments, so the people can no longer "outsource" the work of wisely considering politics and the common good to some distant leaders. The people themselves must become filled with "the spirit of wisdom and understanding, the spirit of counsel and might, the spirit of knowledge and the fear of the LORD."

Voting is the right of every citizen, and, as is always the case with rights, it includes within itself a responsibility—a moral choice and action. Citizens have the responsibility to examine their consciences to consider the moral issues underlying their votes for candidates and issues, as we would for any other important decision. Do we consider justice, based on the rights due in principle to each person? Do we consider the common good—especially the needs of the weakest members of society, such as the poor, the unborn, the sick and aged, and the disabled—or are we acting on prejudices or for selfish ends?

Commonly it is held that religion and politics don't mix, but nothing could be further from the truth. Why would anyone ever intentionally cut God out of the decision-making process in any other part of life? Rejecting God and His commandments becomes morally dangerous, as witnessed by the rise of nationalistic governments that removed God and separated church from state because they feared religion as the "greatest cause of war in history." The two world wars waged by secular nationalistic governments ended up killing thirty-five times as many people as did all the religious wars waged by and among Christians over two thousand years! The atheistic governments of Communist nations killed eighty times as many people as did all the Christian persecutions combined!

Instead of eliminating God, religion, and moral consideration from politics, we need to see public affairs as one of the most important areas of life in which to appeal to the wisdom of the Lord. Politics is where people determine the laws under which the entire society functions; failing to include God's truth, goodness, and wisdom is one factor in the mangling of humanity that occurred throughout the secular twentieth century. Those who reject God's wisdom have themselves to blame when society deteriorates into catastrophic foolishness.

------------------ ❧ ------------------

It is an abomination to kings to do evil, for the throne is estab-lished by righteousness. (Prov. 16:12)

While the voters in a democracy have a great deal of power, the elected and appointed leaders still have special responsibilities. Let us consider two very important reasons for that responsibility that will help us to think about the role of proper moral governance.

First, the decisions made by political leaders affect many people, not only in their own jurisdictions but beyond, and even past national borders. Any evil deeds chosen by politicians are likely to have far greater impact than the sins chosen by most private citizens. When legislators sponsor laws and bills designed to mar-ginalize or harm minority groups and the poor, or when a politician fights for a law to expand abortion or undermine marriage, those actions have an impact on the entire social fabric. For a private citizen to hold immoral opinions or to write mean-spirited letters to the editor is bad enough and still wrong. But when the sins of political leaders change public policy, their sin not only is against charity but is a betrayal of the authority with which they have been entrusted.

This brings us to the second point in this proverb: "the throne is established by righteousness." In other words, all political author-ity ultimately comes from God; it is up to leaders to be righteous stewards of that authority. Americans believe that all political au-thority comes from the people, but ultimately all earthly authority begins with God's divine authority. Therefore, all political leaders have a responsibility to use their power in keeping with God's norms for righteousness, truth, and goodness. Popular injustices against African-Americans, Jews, the unborn, or any other group remain unjust, no matter what popular support the evil measures might have.

Righteousness exalts a nation, but sin is a reproach to any people. (Prov. 14:34)

In 1979, I studied German in Bavaria—a beautiful area with friendly people I enjoyed immensely. Yet the terrible sins of the Nazi era still stung their consciences, and many Germans came up to me to apologize for what had been done, including those who were not even alive at that time. Their penitence and sorrow contained a profound righteousness within it.

One reason they apologized to me is that my family is Polish. Several members of my family helped Jews by hiding them from the Gestapo, and some of my relatives were themselves placed in concentration camps for forced labor, and others were killed. The same was true for other people in our village, Nowa Jastrzabka, as well as for the villages and towns all across Poland and the other occupied countries.

People do well to remember the names of the concentration camps—Auschwitz, Dachau, and the rest—but it would be better that more people knew the names of the many individuals and towns that saved so many other lives. In fact, at the Yad Vashem Memorial to the Holocaust in Jerusalem, the State of Israel commemorates the heroic "Righteous Gentiles" who saved Jews. The rest of the world needs to know their stories because every culture and era needs to be familiar with authentic heroism to inspire righteousness among all ordinary people. Nevertheless, this proverb teaches that the righteous will be exalted by the Lord no matter what the society does, and the sinners will become a reproach.

No nation can look at the horrors of Nazi Germany and say, "Well, at least we aren't as bad as they were." The United States of America and the rest of the world has more than its share of sin that has earned, and will continue to earn, the Lord's reproach. Even when America sent young men to fight Germany and Japan for the sake of freedom, black people could not eat lunch or ride trains with white people across the South — and sometimes could not even vote. That legacy of institutionalized prejudice remains with us into the present and continues to be a reproach for the grave sins of slavery and bigotry. Our obligation is to do everything possible to root out its lasting effects.

Other examples of injustice toward Native Americans, religious minorities, women, children, and others have been and remain present in the world. Sin can become so widely accepted that the structures of society take it for granted, as in the legal system's acceptance of the pornography industry — all the way to the Supreme Court. Over the decades this has become a sex-trade industry in which slavery of women and children has become part of the business. Both individual righteousness in every individual and the reformation of institutions toward righteousness can form a society that truly deserves to be exalted by God.

When the righteous are in authority, the people rejoice; but when the wicked rule, the people groan. (Prov. 29:2)

This saying may seem to be obvious, but closer examination makes things more complicated. Often enough, secular critics of government have no interest in the "righteousness" of leaders and their policies. Secularists challenge believers: "Who are you to say what is righteous and what is wicked?" They want people to aim not at righteousness but at the "greatest good for the greatest number" or some other utilitarian standard.

We believers, however, agree with this proverb: people really want good and righteous government, justice applied equally to all citizens, honest leaders, and lasting peace. Sadly, too few people think that those goods are achievable, so they make unacceptable compromises with immorality. They even start to think that righteousness does not matter, so long as they each get what they want from public policy—or as long as people they do not like are excluded. Catholics sometimes even give up on the most basic tenets of Catholic teaching because it just doesn't seem realistic.

The most tragic example of this is abortion—the worst injustice in our society. Many Catholics and other Christians turn a blind eye to the wickedness in our government and society, especially when it is not popular or respectable to point out that wickedness. A poignant image of the "groaning" of the people under the rule of the wicked is found in the 1984 film *Silent Scream*, which included an ultrasound of an abortion being committed. The little child reacts to the knife by pushing away at it and kicking it, and opening its mouth in protest and pain.

When the wicked rule, the powerless always groan the most. That is human nature: when we turn away from God, our first move is to ignore or, worse, to take advantage of the weak. And who could be weaker than the unborn? We might not be able to hear their groans, but they are just as real and morally important as anyone else's. And it should make us groan, too. Violence and oppression against the weak in any form should make every person cry out for change. We need to find it within ourselves to work for the changes needed to form a truly righteous nation. It might not seem like it now, but the people will truly rejoice when righteousness reigns.

CHAPTER 6

God and Government

The Old Testament teaches that the Lord does not view political issues as isolated from religion. In Exodus, Leviticus, and especially Deuteronomy, the laws of the Lord guide both religious and civil life. For instance, public officials are warned not to accept bribes. The public assemblies and the law courts belonged as much to God's sphere of activity as did worship and sacrifice. The book of Proverbs takes the same perspective.

This discussion takes on a unique aspect in the American context. We often hear about a "wall of separation" between church and state, but that phrase first entered American politics from a letter of Thomas Jefferson assuring a religious congregation that the new constitution would protect them from federal interference, not vice versa. "Separation of church and state," as we now popularly understand it, is a much more modern invention; to be precise, it comes from a 1947 Supreme Court opinion by Justice Hugo Black.

Justice Black would later go on, in 1962, to declare prayer in public schools unconstitutional (*Engel v. Vitale*). But it was that 1947 opinion, *Everson v. Board of Education*, that laid the legal groundwork. The decision in *Everson* permitted a New Jersey school district's program of reimbursing public-transportation costs for students in both public *and religious* schools. But in his opinion, Justice Black introduced a new doctrine: the language "Congress shall make no law respecting an establishment of religion" would apply no longer just to Congress, as the amendment clearly says, but to state and local governments as well.

Since then, the language of "separation of church and state" has taken on a life of its own, with activist organizations expanding its meaning further and further in order to exclude all religious convictions and practices from politics and the public square in general. This completely secular understanding of public life would be as foreign to the first generation of Americans as would the federal establishment of a national religion. Further, this exclusion of God from government and public life would be foreign to the sages of the book of Proverbs and to the Church throughout her history.

While the American tradition of protecting religious practice from state interference is excellent, the artificial separation of politics from faith is not. Christians do not exclude any part of life from God's purview. His moral demands impact government and every other area of our lives. We all answer to God—including legislators, judges, bureaucrats and presidents. We can consider some proverbs on the role of God in government in light of those principles.

⸺⸺⸺ ❦ ⸺⸺⸺

The king's heart is a stream of water in the hand of the LORD; he turns it wherever he will. (Prov. 21:1)

This proverb is a reminder that no matter how powerful a ruler is—even an ancient Israelite king, with near total control over the government—ultimately it is the Lord who is in charge. When the Lord decides to bend a king's (or a president's) heart, it can't be resisted. This is a reminder of the importance of praying for our leaders, that God might turn their hearts toward justice for all—especially the weakest, such as the poor and the unborn.

Now, this doesn't mean that all rulers will be good—far from it! Even the Israelite kings, who had more or less a direct line to God Himself, were often terrible. As a matter of fact, over the course of many centuries, only about half a dozen kings are considered "good," and even they weren't always all that good. King David committed adultery and murder. King Solomon was very wise, but he had a thousand wives and built temples to the idols worshiped by some of those women. The other "good" kings were Asa, Jehoshaphat, Hezekiah, Josiah, but none of them were perfect either.

What this proverb asserts is that there is always a higher authority than the ruler. The Israelite kings who disobeyed God experienced punishment in this world, such as an early death, loss of the throne, or even the destruction of the entire kingdom by foreign invaders. The study of the religious history of the kings of Israel and Judah can teach modern leaders who disobey God today that they, too, will experience punishment in this world or in the next, or in both.

History is filled with autocratic and vicious rulers, with the twentieth century providing the most violent dictators in human history — Hitler, Tojo, Stalin, Mao Tse Tung, Pol Pot, and numerous others. Although such dictators seem powerful enough to direct all aspects of government and society, God can still, if He chooses, dictate to the dictator, as is seen in the collapse of the governments and systems that the twentieth-century dictators established: the "thousand year Reich" of Hitler, the empire of Japan, and the atheistic "workers' paradise" of Soviet Communism have all collapsed under their own wickedness and self-destruction.

All earthly authority has a heavenly basis. This proverb is, in a sense, a presaging of this exchange between Jesus and Pilate: "Pilate therefore said to him, 'You will not speak to me? Do you not know that I have power to release you, and power to crucify you?' Jesus answered him, 'You would have no power over me unless it had been given you from above'" (John 19:10–11). The secularist political forces in the United States and other Western democracies need to learn this lesson as their birth rates and populations decline as fast as their church attendance.

---

*A king who sits on the throne of judgment winnows all evil with
his eyes.* (Prov. 20:8)

The key to this proverb is the word *winnows*. Winnowing is the
process of isolating edible grains of wheat from the light chaff that
flies away in the wind. This proverb reminds us of John the Baptist's
announcement of the coming of the Messiah: "His winnowing fork
is in his hand, and he will clear his threshing floor and gather his
wheat into the granary, but the chaff he will burn with unquench-
able fire" (Matt. 3:12).

The ancient Israelites didn't have a concept of the separation
of powers in government. The king made laws, enforced laws, and
interpreted laws. This proverb refers especially to the role of the
king as the final judge — the adjudicator of last resort, much like
our Supreme Court. A good judge, therefore, acts in a limited sense
as God, because he is tasked with discerning right and wrong, in-
nocence or guilt, in particular situations based on the civil law and
the divine law.

This is another sense in which earthly authority — in this case,
the authority to punish wrongdoing — is a reflection of God's authority. A judge or system of justice has that authority only inasmuch
as God grants it, and it is the judge's or the system's responsibility
to exercise that authority in accordance with God's moral will and
just law. To fail gravely in this regard is in some sense to lose that
grant of authority from the Lord.

A classic example of a court losing its moral bearings is the Supreme Court's *Dred Scott* decision of March 1857. In the majority
decision, Chief Justice Roger B. Taney declared that blacks, whether
slave or free, were not and could never become citizens of the United
States because of the inherent inferiority of the African race. Taney
believed that the framers of the Constitution held that blacks "had

no rights which the white man was bound to respect; and that the negro might justly and lawfully be reduced to slavery for his benefit. He was bought and sold and treated as an ordinary article of merchandise and traffic, whenever profit could be made by it."

Since Dred Scott was black, he was not a citizen and had no right to sue for anything, let alone his freedom. Taney denied that the phrase "all men are created equal" in the Declaration of Independence could apply to blacks: "It is too clear for dispute, that the enslaved African race were not intended to be included, and formed no part of the people who framed and adopted this declaration." The court also declared the 1820 Missouri Compromise unconstitutional, resulting in slavery being permitted in every U.S. territory.

While the popes had clearly, explicitly, and repeatedly taught that Africans had an inherent dignity as human beings redeemed by Jesus Christ and therefore no one had the authority to turn them into slaves (Pope Eugene IV in 1435, Pope Paul III in 1533, Urban VIII in 1639, Benedict XIV in 1741, Pius VII in 1815, Gregory XVI in 1839, and Leo XIII in 1880), the Supreme Court, the businesspeople who profited from slavery, the Democratic Party, and many others all got it gravely wrong. The nation's most violent war, the Civil War, was fought in part over this issue, and slavery was finally ended by the Thirteenth Amendment. This shows, however, that the principles and laws of God must determine how our society is run.

Many seek the favor of a ruler, but from the LORD *a man gets justice. (Prov. 29:26)*

We all, at some point or another, seek favor from an authority figure. Sometimes this is harmless, even good and important, such as appealing to get a bureaucratic error fixed or some other wrong righted. Sometimes it's not so harmless, such as lobbying for legislation that would serve personal or corporate interests while hurting the common good.

The key distinction here is between "favor" and "justice." The proverb acknowledges that we seek favor from earthly authorities without passing judgment on that fact. But it also suggests that "justice" is a much worthier goal, all things considered, than "favor." We should not content ourselves with the fleeting approval of a governor or a legislator; our primary goal must always be the justice that is defined by the Lord and His Church.

I'm reminded here of a friend who would switch political parties not based on any principle of justice or the common good, but based on which party would be easier to gain influence in. That's prioritizing earthly favor and power over God's justice. We must base our political decisions on the timeless teachings of Christ and the Church, rather than the always-changing dynamics of partisan politics.

The poor man and the oppressor meet together; the LORD gives light to the eyes of both. (Prov. 29:13)

In this short proverb there is a radical idea: the equal dignity of all men and women before God. Throughout history various groups, especially the poor and "common" people, have been considered "less" than their rulers, or "betters." But this one sentence explodes that idea, reminding us that regardless of our station in this life, "the Lord gives light to [our] eyes"— in other words, He given each person life. Our first relationship is always with Him, and so our first duty is always to Him.

This insight is so important whenever we think about the rich and the poor, the powerful and the weak, the well-connected and the marginalized. For all the terrible things we might think about those who use their power to oppress and impoverish other people, we must remember that they are children of God and can, with His grace, change and convert. And for all the pity we might have toward the poor and the victimized, we must remember that they are children of God and deserve to be treated as such, not turned into symbols or treated like infants who can do nothing for themselves.

The poor include as many intelligent and energetic people as do the rich or middle class, and respect for their dignity includes opening up opportunities for them to succeed in education, business, politics, and all the other areas of human endeavor. Our duty as wise Christian citizens is to ensure that the government treats each person, as a child of God, with equal dignity, and then to look for ways to help all citizens find opportunities for freedom, success, and personal development.

God is the first and supreme Authority, so all political authority ultimately comes from Him. He is also the first and supreme Being, and so everything and everyone that exists comes from Him. What does this mean for our thinking about government?

In his sermon "The Weight of Glory," C. S. Lewis gave a very profound reflection on governments and civilizations: all governments fall; all nations fall. The great empires of the past have all collapsed, and other powers have come and gone. In France they have had monarchy and democracy, tyranny and feudalism. In Russia they have had monarchy, tyranny, oligarchy, and a certain amount of democracy; the United States has been under a monarchy, colonial assemblies, and a democratic republic, founded by revolution and nearly destroyed by civil war. Political parties had risen and fallen — how many Americans even remember the Whig Party?

But what lasts in a society? Its people. You and I are the ones who will outlast the ages. Every person around you will live forever.

One of the most basic facts of life is that governments are mortal, but each and every human person is immortal. God created every person to live with Him forever, and He desires to raise everyone from the dead, so as to "shine like the sun" (see Dan. 12:3). Those who reject Him and His ways will also be raised to eternal life, but they will become "everlasting horrors" (see Dan. 12:2). There will be a time when we are judged by God as to whether we deserve Heaven or Hell. At that moment we will look back on having lived in the United States as a long-ago dream. Remembering this is a way to keep our relationship with politics, culture, and our country in God's perspective. These things pass away; only He endures. God willing, we will be there with Him.

CHAPTER 7

Wealth and Poverty

Sacred Scripture, including the book of Proverbs, has much to say about wealth and poverty. The sages were especially concerned with the treatment of the poor by the powerful, as well as with the wise use of possessions for their authentic purposes. In this chapter we'll consider a prayer and three proverbs that shed light on the ways of thinking about excess and want, both in our lives and in the society around us.

Two things I ask of you; do not deny them to me before I die: Remove far from me falsehood and lying; give me neither poverty nor riches; feed me with the food that I need, or I shall be full, and deny you, and say, "Who is the LORD?" or I shall be poor, and steal, and profane the name of my God. (Prov. 30:7–9)

Chapter 30 in the book of Proverbs is known as the "Words of Agur." Agur, son of Jakeh, may have been a foreigner to the land of Israel, but his wisdom was renowned and has been passed down through this Israelite book. Proverbs 30:7–9 is known as "Agur's Prayer," in which he asks two things of the Lord: that he not fall into the world of falsehood, and that he be neither rich nor poor. We will focus on the second petition.

In our culture, enough is never enough. We're supposed to always want more than we have. It's like Lake Wobegon from Garrison Keillor's *Prairie Home Companion*, where "all the children are above average." No one wants to be just average because it is considered a failure of competence or ambition. Our commercials tell us that we need and deserve luxuries, fantastic cars, strong trucks, and sexy clothing. They do not merely assert that we need these things; they help to invent a need for them.

The prayer of Agur expresses the spiritual dangers of having more than enough, as well as of not having enough. Both material plenty and material poverty are challenges to our relationship with the Lord. On the one hand, when we are surrounded by goodies, we can easily become self-indulgent and self-satisfied, forgetting our reliance on the Lord. Not only are we tempted to forget Him because we no longer have to ask Him for sustenance—that is, "our daily bread"—but we also forget that what we have was ultimately given to us by Him. We want to believe that our riches all come from our own work and cleverness and diligence, rather than from the Lord. After all, who invented silver and gold: humans or God? All that humans know how to do is find gold, smelt it, and fashion it into something beautiful or useful.

Poverty, however, comes with spiritual challenges as well. Agur says that if he were poor, he would be tempted to "profane the name of my God" by breaking the commandment that forbids stealing. Furthermore, the difficulties of poverty might drive him into despair and cursing the Lord for his troubles. Poverty is not romantic, as can be seen in the sickness, hunger, and other deprivations suffered by the poor. The Lord has a special love for the poor, but that does not mean that poverty is always spiritually uplifting. It comes with as many temptations as riches do, just different and less expensive ones.

Therefore, Agur prays, as we should as well, just to have enough. St. Ignatius of Loyola, the founder of the Jesuits, also asks us to seek neither riches nor poverty, neither long life nor short life, neither health nor sickness; rather pray for the strength to seek only what God wants and to ask only what He would have us do for His "greater glory." The best way to avoid the temptations that come with various material situations of riches or poverty is to maintain a prayerful relationship with the Lord and seek His guidance to reach His glory.

Do not remove an ancient landmark or encroach on the fields of orphans, for their redeemer is strong; he will plead their cause against you. (Prov. 23:10–11)

This proverb requires a bit of explanation. The ancient Israelites believed that the land of Israel literally belonged to God. It was His hereditary portion of the earth. In the book of Joshua (chapters 13–21), the Lord instructed Joshua to set up boundaries for parcels of land for each tribe, clan, and family; the boundaries were marked with piles of stones as landmarks. The Israelites accepted these parcels of land as gifts given to them directly by the Lord, and they passed them down through the generations so that each family could have enough land to grow their food and raise their cattle.

In that light, the first part of this proverb forbids any attempt to adjust the land distribution or take for oneself the land that God had apportioned for other families. Moving a landmark, whether to add more land to one's own portion or to take land away from a hated enemy, was forbidden. Adjusting other people's heritage was a serious interference in the Lord's plan for His people and an infringement of the covenantal promise to grant them the Promised Land. Some people might try to reason that God's plan seems unfair, but their judgment of the matter does not permit them to apply their own, often selfish, reasoning to justify stealing another person's heritage in contravention of His will.

The second part of the proverb is the more relevant to our consideration of the rich and the poor. If the father of a family died before his children had grown up, which was not uncommon in times past, the land and the other property of the orphans would be vulnerable to confiscation by the more powerful members of the community. In ancient societies, having an adult man as the protector of the family was absolutely necessary. Without such strong protectors, wealthier and more powerful landholders could swoop in and take the land of families who were helpless, as was frequently condemned by the Law, the prophets, and the sages:

> You shall not afflict any widow or orphan. If you do afflict them, and they cry out to me, I will surely hear their cry; and my wrath will burn, and I will kill you with the sword, and your wives shall become widows and your children fatherless. (Exod. 22:22–24)
>
> Then I will draw near to you for judgment; I will be a swift witness against the sorcerers, against the adulterers, against those who swear falsely, against those who oppress the hireling in his wages, the widow and the orphan, against those who thrust aside the sojourner, and do not fear me, says the LORD of hosts. (Mal. 3:5)

Still, the final message of the proverb is that the poor and the unfortunate are not ultimately helpless: the Lord is their protector or "redeemer." The Lord considers the violation of the dignity and the rights of the helpless so severe that He Himself will intervene as their counselor. This statement is echoed in those sins that the Church traditionally teaches "cry to heaven" for vengeance: "the cry of the foreigner, the widow, and the orphan [and] injustice to the wage earner" (CCC 1867). The Lord personally intervenes on behalf of the most helpless, whether in this life or in the next, because He takes oppression of the poor very seriously.

Today there are many ways in which the poor are victimized by various parts of society. Although a college education is necessary to do well in the contemporary economy, society fails to provide the excellent or even adequate primary and secondary education for the poor that make college a real possibility. Predatory loan companies squeeze high interest rates out of those who struggle from paycheck to paycheck, making it impossible for such borrowers ever to get out of debt. Unjust employers often do not pay full-time workers enough for survival. Politicians take bribes and kickbacks that affect their willingness to help the urban poor, while at the same time taking their votes for granted. All of these evils fall within the message of this proverb, so everyone should beware: as helpless as the poor may seem, the Lord "will plead their cause" on Judgment Day. On the Day of Judgment we all want to be among the "sheep," who came to the aid of the hungry, the thirsty, the naked, the imprisoned, and the sick, finding Jesus Christ in each of them, rather than be counted among the "goats," who missed Christ in the poor and ended in Hell (see Matt. 25:31–46).

Wealth brings many new friends, but a poor man is deserted by his friend. (Prov. 19:4)

Many stories about people who win the lottery tell of the ways they are bombarded with requests from distant relatives and from people they met once many years ago asking to "reconnect." One has less a sense of newfound familial love than the same old greed among those who simply want a piece of those winnings. The sages recognized this phenomenon long ago: when you are rich, everyone wants to be your friend.

But no one gets much benefit from befriending the poor—at least nothing material. All too often, one of the terrible conditions that accompanies poverty is loneliness. In the book of Job we read of Job's friends abandoning him when his fortunes are destroyed by catastrophes and he is afflicted with a foul sickness. The three friends who do come to console him actually cause him more grief by blaming him for his troubles. Even his wife speaks like the foolish women by telling him to "curse God, and die" (Job 2:9). Why does this happen?

Frequently, the friendless poor do not have a support network to help them get by. The people around them worry that the poverty will never end, especially if the person is sick or old. All too often they end up poor not just in material things, but in healthy relationships with people who love them for themselves and just as they are. Loneliness and abandonment only add to the temptation to despair.

The frequency of such phenomena should encourage us to reflect: How do I think of my relationships? Are they ways to get things for myself, or do I really care about the good of my friends more than myself? How can I improve my relationships? How can I be a true friend to others in need—especially those poor in both money and in friendship? There is, for instance, an all-too-common pattern by which people give things or do things to get people to love them. (In their early years the Beatles warned the world: "Can't buy me love.") The person who tries to purchase love through gifts or actions eventually runs out of things to give away. If the love of others is given in response to gifts, big or small, the takers will leave the givers alone and lonely because they knew that the gifts were dependent on neediness rather than on love. Once the gifts are gone, so are the takers.

How do we become wise in regard to loving the poor? Since the 1960s, the federal government has distributed trillions of dollars in programs to the poor and some of that has resulted in certain financial improvements—for instance, the availability of electricity, water, sanitation, and other services increased dramatically in the rural South during the 1960s. On the other hand, the percentage of poor city dwellers has not improved nearly enough. Partly in response to the present structure of government welfare programs, too many people remain stuck in government housing with little economic opportunity, either for work or for development of their own businesses.

The families of the poor have also broken down so badly that more than half of Hispanic babies and about 73 percent of African-American babies are born to unwed parents. Only 19 percent of black children live with their mother and father. Such family instability becomes the strongest indicator of the children's failure to finish high school and of the likelihood that the daughters will become unwed mothers (about 60 percent), and that the children will abuse drugs and go to prison (80 to 85 percent of all inmates are the children of unmarried parents, regardless of race or ethnicity).

Where is the path of wisdom in helping the poor? Obviously it takes money, but it is not to be found only in giving money. Giving time and attention to the poor — tending to their deeper needs and concerns — is key. The poor understand much about their own environment, whether it is rural or urban, and they have much to teach those who would help them. They have important insights on ways to handle a life radically different from what most middle-class Americans have known.

Furthermore, the experiences and connections of the wealthier members of society, along with some governmental aid, can be brought to bear to improve the situations of poverty in more lasting ways. Too often government programs are designed primarily to elect politicians. How can the poor find economic independence and security, freed from governmental limitations, such as maximum incomes for public-housing residents. The wise will seek the deeper needs for strengthening family bonds so that the children know that their father and mother are irreplaceable, and that they, as children, are unique, dignified, and irreplaceable in the eyes of their parents. The wise will go beyond giving things to the poor but will make possible the development of business, opportunity, education, and skill development that make the poor independent enough to care for themselves and their families.

When the wise seek these and other thoughtful developments, truly the poor will end up having taught them more than they taught the poor.

Whoever is kind to the poor lends to the LORD, and will be repaid in full. (Prov. 19:17)

A perfect way to close out this chapter is with a reflection on the Lord's involvement in the process of improving the lives of the poor. Just as the Lord will ultimately vindicate the rights of the poor when they are victimized, so also will He reward those who are wise and generous to the poor. This promise may make it easier for people of means to become emotionally and spiritually detached from their money and other possessions. Instead of thinking that the things around us are ours to use in any way that we please, we can see that all the money and possessions we have are given to our care. These things will not be ours forever, one way or another. I have never seen a hearse with a luggage rack or a trailer hitch.

This ought to remind us that all the things around us pass on to others—whether to the trash heap, to one's heirs (or the government), or to the people who surround us, including the poor. Again, generous distribution of one's goods should be done wisely, with an aim to the greater good and the deeper human needs of the poor. Generosity is not primarily oriented to making the giver feel good about himself but is concerned with the good of the receiver.

At the same time, the perspective of the sage in this proverb is that one's gifts to the poor are not a loss but rather a kind of loan to the Lord. Even this perspective omits the sense that the Lord gave everyone on earth all the gifts that they have in their possession. Therefore, generosity to those in need, whether through time or material gifts, is actually a return back to the original Giver — the Lord God Himself. This proverb teaches us that the Lord's repayment to the generous giver is ensured, whether in this life or in the next. Along these same lines our Lord Jesus taught us:

> Do not lay up for yourselves treasures on earth, where moth and rust consume and where thieves break in and steal, but lay up for yourselves treasures in heaven, where neither moth nor rust consumes and where thieves do not break in and steal. For where your treasure is, there will your heart be also. (Matt. 6:19–21)

Of course, there are many stories of people whose generosity with the poor has been repaid in this life. Unpredictable things happen — gifts, inheritances, raises in wages, and so on — that replace the things individuals had given away. However, the lesson is not to stop and count the newfound wealth, but to see it as a new opportunity to become more generous in ever cleverer and wiser ways.

Like any other virtue, generosity to the poor is a habit, and the most difficult part of any good habit is to begin living it. Today is the day everyone can decide to start (or to continue) the hard work of developing a habit of generosity. The joy of giving overcomes any fear of losing, and ultimately it draws one closer to God our Lord, who promises to be infinitely more generous than any of us could know how to be.

CHAPTER 8

Business and Fairness

It's easy for us to fall into the trap of thinking that Sunday is for God and the rest of the week is for work. After all, our culture teaches us that religion and business are two separate areas of life. But nothing could be further from the truth. As we will see, the Lord cares deeply about commerce and business. Our conduct in the world of business can be part of our sanctification—or it can lead us to condemnation.

A false balance is an abomination to the LORD, but a just weight is his delight. . . . A just balance and scales are the LORD's; all the weights in the bag are his work. (Prov. 11:1; 16:11)

The phrases "false balance" and "just weight" refer to the scales the ancient Israelites used in weighing goods and money for trade. Ancient merchants had bags of weights of different sizes in order to measure large and small items to a reasonable level of precision. Honesty in business transactions, therefore, rested on the accuracy of those weights. An unscrupulous merchant could use improperly marked weights to cheat by using lighter or heavier weights, depending on the advantage he might receive when selling or buying. Archaeologists have found sets of weights from Mesopotamia that had been either hollowed out to be lighter than labeled or filled with lead to be heavier when beneficial.

The sage uses the word *abomination* to make it clear that the Lord finds cheating in business transactions to be particularly appalling. We could go as far as to say that dishonest business practices are disgusting to God, as reflected in later concerns for fairness in the Jewish Talmud, which warns shopkeepers to clean their measures, weights, and scales regularly in order to ensure integrity in business.

Modern people often think and act as if economic concerns are distinct and separate from moral and spiritual concerns. This is the economic equivalent of the idea that religion should not "interfere" with politics. People assume that "everyone pursues self-interest," and morality has nothing, or at least very little, to do with it. However, this proverb teaches that such a secular view of business could not be more wrong.

Business must not be merely concerned with self-interest, and morality requires much more than following the economic and legal rules of a particular society. It's easy to learn enough about business practice and law to stay out of jail—while still treating others in ways that are an "abomination to the Lord." Proverbs 16:11 asserts that honesty and fairness in business belong squarely within God's realm of concern. His standards of righteousness, goodness, and truth apply to everyone and every action—including business practices—at our judgment. Therefore, true wisdom calls for honest business practices to be integrated into the examination of conscience of every person who participates in that area of life.

Prices and wages are good examples of areas where business conduct might be legal, strictly speaking, but possibly gravely immoral. Differences in economic and political power between buyers and sellers, for instance, might make it possible for a company to compel small suppliers, especially in underdeveloped countries, to sell their goods at an unjustly low price. Similarly, a company could take advantage of poor laborers who can't find other work by paying a wage that is legal but still so low that the workers cannot live a decent life. In recent decades, some business leaders have promoted illegal immigration of poor people as a way to keep wages low, while many citizens have difficulty finding jobs that pay a decent wage. While following just rules and regulations may be a first step to fairness in business, authentic justice will rest in the Lord's moral expectations by which the authentic good of workers, customers, and employers are maintained in balance.

The wisdom of Pope St. John Paul II concerning solidarity is applicable here. Christians are not called to isolate groups or individuals into opposing factions, as happens all too often in political discourse. Rather, the principle of solidarity helps everyone understand that all members of society share in the well-being of one another and of the community; therefore, we are to seek what is good for each other. Employers, workers, and customers do well to consider how their cooperation and concern for their mutual benefit can improve everyone's position in society.

Henry Ford understood that only if he paid his workers a decent wage would they be able to purchase the cars he taught them how to make. On the other hand, only when the employees help the company make a profit will they be able to keep their jobs. Furthermore, when businesses manufacture goods or provide services that offer true benefits to the customers, the long-range prospects for the business remains solid. Corporations do well to consider how their products benefit their customers or make life more beautiful so as to provide long-term opportunities for the owners, workers, and customers alike.

Another component of just business practice is the fulfillment people find at their jobs. Of course, most jobs entail a certain amount of occasional drudgery—and some more than others. Yet even when the work is difficult and even strains the body and the mind, it is possible to develop a work environment that makes employees and employers alike look forward to their toil as a meaningful and satisfying part of their lives. Farmers sweat in the heat and shiver in the cold, but they have the joy of making things grow and feeding the world. Job satisfaction flows from a sense of accomplishment, purpose, and especially the feeling of being respected by other people for one's work.

The Son of God became flesh within the womb of a carpenter's betrothed, and He became a carpenter Himself. Therefore He understands the importance of "job satisfaction," and He will bless those who help bring it about for their fellow workers.

Wealth hastily gotten will dwindle, but he who gathers little by little will increase it. . . . An inheritance gotten hastily in the beginning will in the end not be blessed. (Prov. 13:11; 20:21)

On one level these two proverbs simply state common sense. We have all seen get-rich-quick schemes on television, the Internet, and so on. Most people know, even if they are sometimes a bit tempted, that these schemes are usually scams, as the secular proverb states, "If it seems too good to be true, it probably is."

These proverbs remind us of the phenomenon of lottery winners who go bankrupt and experience other personal problems, such as drug abuse. Nearly three out of every four jackpot winners go broke within a decade of their windfall. (The lottery doesn't hold much temptation for me: if I won it, under my Jesuit vows I'd have to turn the winnings in to my provincial!) But this is not just a modern issue: the ancient Israelites knew of people who squandered unexpected fortunes, and they recognized that "hastily gotten" wealth leads to ruin.

Why is that the case? Why is quick wealth not blessed "in the end," while steady earning tends to grow over time? The answer is that managing money is a discipline that requires virtues such as prudence and self-control. Like all virtues, they are developed through habits. Virtues do not appear overnight along with good fortune. They require years, even decades, to build up within each person. Prudence and self-control are taught to the young by people who already live them, and throughout life each person grows in the virtues through discipline. At first, the discipline comes from others, especially parents and teachers; over time, people can develop self-discipline, with help from those close to them who remind them of the need for prudent planning and temperate self-control.

When wealth grows steadily through prudence and hard work, individuals slowly and deeply acquire the virtuous habits necessary for managing possessions. Over time and through experiences of success and failure, one's knowledge and understanding of money, investments, and savings develop along with one's resources. If all goes well, people will acquire the wisdom and discipline to manage their resources at any given time. Clearly, it is best when money and possessions increase as virtue grows: slowly, with the accumulation of good habits.

Hastily gotten wealth, such as inheritances, jackpots, or corporate windfalls, on the other hand, burden the recipients with enormous responsibility and temptation before they have developed the virtues to handle them. Without the prudence to handle sudden increases of money and wealth, people become easy prey for con men and investment scams—as well as for the devil, who could not be more excited to approach an unprepared person bombarded with new types of temptation.

Business and finance aren't about getting as rich as possible as quickly as possible, as a certain secular attitude assumes. Rather, one's first responsibility with all the goods of this world is to the Lord. A great way to keep Him first in one's life is to increase one's fortunes along with, not ahead of, the virtues.

Better is a little with righteousness than great revenues with injustice. (Prov. 16:8)

This proverb addresses a similar theme a bit more directly. Despite what some people in the secular culture might teach, wealth is not in itself the greatest good in life. We can sometimes do good things—for our families, for the poor, for the Church—with wealth, but having a massive bank account does not by itself give anyone credit with the Lord. After all, the whole universe already belongs to Him; why would He be interested in a bank account? With God, righteousness and moral goodness have precedence in His evaluation of human beings.

Righteousness is not the same as bare legality; politicians are happy to legalize immoral behavior, especially if it will protect friends and patrons. Christians are challenged, on the other hand, always to ask themselves about their duties in justice to those who are less powerful. How does one treat subordinates, employees, the poor, the homeless, and so on? If the pursuit of wealth requires one to make other people suffer or to impose hardships on them in order to improve one's own life, then an injustice has been done. The sages admonish everyone to have the self-knowledge and discipline to include the just rights due to a wider group of people when pursuing one's own benefits and wealth.

For that reason, Jesus Christ addressed His disciples on the challenges of wealth when He asked, "For what does it profit a man, to gain the whole world and forfeit his life?" (Mark 8:36). He challenges everyone never to trade eternal life for temporary wealth and power here on earth. Those who seek their happiness in material goods and pleasures in and for this life will enjoy neither the present life nor eternity in Hell. Those who accept His beatitude "Blessed are the poor in spirit, for theirs is the kingdom of heaven" (Matt. 5:3), will find peace in this life and in the next as well.

------------------- ❁ -------------------

Poverty and disgrace come to him who ignores instruction, but he who heeds reproof is honored. (Prov. 13:18)

Modern society admires the inventor or entrepreneur who creates something and builds a business with nothing but his own cleverness. But those who have actually designed inventions and built businesses will gladly explain that they did not achieve their accomplishments all alone. The ancient sage behind this proverb teaches that relying solely on one's intuitions while ignoring the advice and help of others may work once every thousand times, but it usually leads to failure. The most successful people learn from those with the wisdom of experience, particularly when other people's advice challenges or contradicts their own thinking.

Whether in business or in growing in holiness, success is a collaborative venture. At the very beginning of creation the Lord said, "It is not good that the man should be alone" (Gen. 2:18). Working and living together is part of being human. This is true not only of the need for a spouse, but in business it points to the need for the guidance of mentors in all areas of life. The other side of this principle is the willingness to be generous in serving others when our wisdom could be helpful to them. Working together to make a business prosper for the benefit of inventors, employers, employees, and customers is just another way to view the solidarity that makes the world more just and prosperous. Solidarity in these practical areas of life may even help to prepare one another for the new life in Heaven.

PART 3

Virtue

CHAPTER 9

Anger and Timidity

Anger comes up often in the book of Proverbs, not just because there has always been so much of it in the world, but because getting it right is so important. Our culture tends to look at anger as always being dangerous, but that's not how the wisdom writers saw it. Anger can become quite dangerous when it is uncontrolled and isolated from sound reasoning, but anger can also be an important tool for improving the world. The sages offer some important insights on the role of anger.

He who is slow to anger has great understanding, but he who has a hasty temper exalts folly. (Prov.14:29)

The first thing to notice about this proverb is the phrase "slow to anger." The wisdom writer is not praising the person who never gets angry; rather, he is praising the patient person who has control of his anger. Understanding comes, at least in part, from a healthy relationship with anger.

Now, the patient person doesn't just bottle up anger until it explodes. That isn't healthy, and it certainly does not demonstrate control over the passion of anger. Neither does understanding come from just waiting for the boiling point, then blowing up at the unlucky person who triggers our anger at some unexpected moment. Instead, understanding comes from having the patience to wait and see what the appropriate response to a situation will be.

A person grows in understanding by asking pertinent questions: What did someone do to make me angry in this particular situation? Why might this person have acted in such a frustrating way? Why might he or she be justifiably angry *with me*? What other circumstances have contributed to this situation? Should I adjust my expectations or assumptions as much as (or more than) the other person needs to adjust his or her behavior or attitude?

Understanding the answers to these questions does not necessarily mean that we should never get angry. Rather, it means that we should grant others the sympathy and consideration we would expect them to give us. We can all think of situations in which we did something that appeared totally justified to us but insulted or affronted a friend, colleague, or family member. Leaping immediately into anger often causes the confusion and misunderstanding by which we "exalt folly," making it more difficult to resolve the problems at hand.

The wise are able to guide and direct the passion of anger by keeping it under the control of reasonable reflection on the situation. When anger and passion take control of a people, they fall into foolishness. When reason is in charge, they learn to deploy anger wisely and to become people of true understanding.

------------------------------❖------------------------------

A soft answer turns away wrath, but a harsh word stirs up anger.
(Prov. 15:1)

In Hebrew, the word that we translate as "wrath" also refers to heat, so an ancient reader would have immediately recognized the comparison between the danger of heat and of the uncontrolled anger of wrath. As fire can be controlled by removing wind and air, so can we calm another's wrath with cool calmness and understanding.

Remember from the first proverb in this chapter that uncontrolled anger is "folly." Although the wise person responds to anger with the coolness of reason and reflection, folly does not always respond to wisdom. Therefore, the wise person does well to be prepared for ongoing foolishness from a person bent on anger. Wisdom might even demand a righteous and controlled anger in response, such as Jesus Christ expressed when He drove out the money changers from the Temple (Matt. 21:12–13). This kind of controlled anger is certainly better than throwing fuel on the fire with our own "harsh words." On another occasion, as Jesus' opponents watched whether He would heal a man with a withered hand so that they could accuse him of profaning the Sabbath, he "looked around at them with anger, grieved at their hardness of heart." He then healed the man and left the area, while his enemies plotted "to destroy him." He left the area and healed people elsewhere on that occasion (Mark 3:1–8).

Once in the late 1960s, while I was a novice working with gangs in a dangerous inner-city neighborhood, I was confronted by a group of people including two local politicians, two policemen, and a couple of others with crime-syndicate connections. I had been working with a Saul Alinsky–inspired community-organizing group; a combination of efforts against local landlords and the city housing authority, plus increased gang activity had upset these mob-connected folks. For hours they shouted and screamed at me as I sat among them. All I did was look directly into their eyes, stare at them, and answer politely. After three or four hours they calmed down, and even came to respect the fact that I calmly looked directly at them. Of course, inside I was quite scared, and my knees were literally shaking! But that encounter became my prime experience of living out the truth that "a harsh word stirs up anger." I did not see any need to make these people angrier!

———————————❧———————————

For pressing milk produces curds, pressing the nose produces blood, and pressing anger produces strife. (Prov. 30:33)

This descriptive proverb gives us some memorable and even humorous images, but its point is important: the natural result of intentionally provoking anger is further discord. The word "strife" in Hebrew also refers to lawsuits, so an extra meaning here is that "pressing anger" turns others — even friends — into adversaries, including within the law court. This is especially relevant in our overly litigious society.

It is simply disrespectful to the dignity of other people to try intentionally to anger them. It tempts them to give control of their will and decision-making over to the passion of anger, inducing them to lose their temper rather than keep it in control. Provoking people to anger makes a game out of their reactions and treats them as something to be played with, rather than as a person. Inducing another person to sin is itself a sin. That explains why provocation leads to the division of communities into opposing factions, as is increasingly the case among politicians and their partisans in the media.

We all know that children, particularly siblings, love to press each other's buttons. Part of growing up is learning that those behaviors are selfish and destructive; as St. Paul says, we are to put an end to childish things (see 1 Cor. 13:11). Kids can work through that "strife" pretty easily, since their memories are short and their friendships are durable. As they get older, though, those petty behaviors become increasingly destructive. Adults do well to heed the wisdom from this proverb and from St. Paul: it isn't worthwhile to provoke anger intentionally, even if one tries to wiggle out of the situation by claiming to have just been joking all along. It seems, in fact, that the sages rejected that cheap dodge almost three millennia ago, as we will see in our next proverb.

———————⬡———————

Like a madman who throws firebrands, arrows, and death, is the man who deceives his neighbor and says, "I am only joking!" (Prov. 26:18–19)

This proverb demonstrates how timeless our patterns of speech are, and how perceptive the sages were! Across thousands of years and in thousands of different languages, people throughout history have tried to avoid responsibility for their deceits and tricks by telling others, "I was just kidding!" Sometimes the use of this excuse after deceiving someone is yet one more lie that is meant to cover the tracks of the earlier deception. However, piling lies on top of one another simply makes the sin and its damage worse, and it can make the tangle of falsehoods so complicated that one can never extricate himself from them.

Even if the intent is not to hurt others with the deceit—for example, even if a person really was only joking—it is still reckless behavior, like throwing matches around an oil refinery. The great insight of this proverb stems from the idea that the liar—the "madman who throws firebrands"—might really not intend to hurt anybody. That does not, however, change the fact that his recklessness is dangerous. It is impossible to undo that first deceit, and as a result its consequences, like a flung arrow or a thrown match, are out of our control. The initial deceiver is still responsible for those consequences, since he so carelessly let loose risky lies to begin with.

A classic example of this occurred in 1967, when the Soviets told the Arab nations surrounding Israel that spy satellites showed that the Israelis were massing troops near their borders. The Israelis denied the claim and invited observers to see that it was not true, but the Arabs believed the Soviets anyway. Arab armies began to gather near the borders, and in response the Israelis massed their own troops. On June 5, the Israelis launched an attack, and a week later they had pushed back all the opposing armies and gained control of large swaths of Egypt, Jordan, and Syria. Thousands died and millions of dollars of equipment was destroyed, including the U.S.S. *Liberty*, an American communications ship that was bombed by the Israelis. All of this was due to the deceit of the Arabs by their Soviet ally. Other such examples could be drawn from world history and personal experience, backing up the truth of ancient Israelite wisdom.

He who winks the eye causes trouble, but he who boldly reproves makes peace. (Prov. 10:10)

This proverb indicates the importance of controlled, justified anger. The inability to muster justified anger can be just as much a problem as is uncontrolled anger. In fact, in our people-pleasing society the neglect of justified anger may be *more* of a problem than is too much anger. Some people are so invested in having proper politically correct attitudes and avoiding ruffling the feathers of badly behaving people that they refrain from boldly representing the truth of what God had revealed and demanded for society and for individuals. The sages had in their minds that people-pleasing, indulgent attitude when they wrote the phrase, "he who winks the eye."

When faced with terrible injustices and everyday bad behavior, it seems easier to give that wink of the eye—a subtle suggestion of approval—rather than to take action against obnoxious behavior. For instance, in politics, too many officials and citizens wink their eyes at the corruption of officeholders because at this point we expect such malfeasance. The corrupt politician might be very likable in other ways—due either to personality or policy promises. Experience shows, however, that when we attempt to keep the peace by failing to intervene, bad situations only get worse—corruption and graft, for instance, become more and more normalized.

Even so, it remains very difficult to find the courage to reprove and challenge wrongdoers. Particularly in recent years, people are so afraid to be perceived as "judgmental" that they refuse to condemn evil behavior clearly. They forget that winking at sin and evil gives it permission to gain a foothold in our common life, and then it becomes more difficult to eradicate. Another example from history was the march of the German army into the Rhineland before World War II. The Allies had ordered the German army to stay out of the Rhineland as part of the Treaty of Versailles, but when Hitler ordered his army to enter that territory, the Allies winked and did nothing. This winking continued throughout Hitler's initial rise to power in Europe, including the annexation of Austria and the invasion of Czechoslovakia. On September 1, 1939, the Germans invaded Poland, and the Allies became embroiled in a world war that cost them far more lives and material than they would have lost had they simply confronted Hitler a couple of years earlier in the Rhineland.

People use a number of clichés to justify letting bad things continue to happen in everyday life: "different strokes for different folks"; "whatever floats your boat"; "You do your thing, and I'll do my thing." Certainly, at times, wisdom and prudence demand tolerance of things we do not particularly like. Wisdom, however, helps one learn when the greater good of the other person, as well as the common good, demands a "bold reproof." One must think carefully about the criteria that make certain issues very important while others are less significant.

For instance, parents often struggle with finding ways to respond to serious misbehavior in their children. Spilled milk is nothing, but bullying, drug and alcohol abuse, and sexual misconduct and irresponsibility are very serious problems. Parents have to step up to the plate and correct these issues, sometimes with a gentle word, and at other times with controlled but serious anger at bad behavior. Parents do their children no good by obscuring the truth of God's expectations about right and wrong, truth and falsehood, and good and evil merely to maintain the appearance of being "cool." As the Lord says, "No one after lighting a lamp puts it under the bushel basket" (see Matt. 5:15). We owe our children the light of the truth, not the darkness of ignorance for the sake of a false and short-lived "peace."

On the other hand, a "bold reproof" does not require us to attack the *person* who committed the misbehavior. In fact, using anger as a way to reject the perpetrator of wrong or wicked actions will easily turn into an occasion of uncontrolled wrath. Judging others as unworthy of love or as inherently flawed leads to another form of folly. When correcting someone's bad behavior, we must be thoughtful and precise in our criticism and make sure that we direct our anger at the vice or the sinful action in question. We must continue to cherish the person and demonstrate that we truly want what is best for him, and that includes helping him to root out evil that harms him and those around him. We are always to love that person and to recognize his value.

When correcting children, for instance, wise parents will prepare a plan of action, not just a shout here and a holler there, that corrects the child through long-term formation. This can include both stating the punishment that will be meted out for certain bad behaviors as well as taking time to draw the chastened child back to an embrace and tender acceptance. Children fully expect to be punished for misbehavior, and often they do naughty things in such a way as to get caught. On one level, they want to see if their parents will follow through on earlier threats and chastise their misbehavior, or whether their parents are merely talkers who do not act on their own warnings. Also, they want to see if the punishment will be just what was threatened, or more (or less) than the warning, or totally arbitrary; in other words, they are sensitive to fairness.

In the end, as the proverb says, the parents who warn their children about upcoming punishment for predictable misbehavior, and then follow through with thoughtful correction intermixed with loving acceptance (of the children, not of the misbehavior), will find true peace. Peace comes from following God's will with integrity, and children who are corrected justly, punished fairly, and yet are loved unconditionally will grow up with greater security and peace than those who either run wild with no discipline or those whose discipline and correction has no consistency or principle to it.

CHAPTER 10

Pride and Humility

Genesis 3 tells of the Serpent's temptation of Adam and Eve. Beyond the attractiveness of the "fruit of the knowledge of good and evil" in sight and taste, the temptation behind their interest in the fruit appealed to their pride: "You will be like God" (Gen. 3:5–6). Few can see, then, that from the very beginning in the Garden of Eden, human beings have tried to go it alone and live as if only their own ideas, considerations, and efforts really mattered. They want to succeed in every realm of life, from business and politics to growing in holiness, solely by their own efforts. That temptation, however, typically involves not only ignoring and subordinating fellow human beings to the prideful pursuit of one's own success, but also ignoring and subordinating God Himself.

Pride and arrogance are vices that persist throughout human history, as the proverbs teach us. The ancient sages recognize the same dangers of pride (and the benefits of humility) that even secular culture sometimes recognizes today. The difference between proverbial wisdom and secular philosophies is the prescription for correcting the sin of pride. The proverbs recommend knowing, loving, and fearing the Lord; only in Him can we avoid the pitfalls of pride. Secular society optimistically proposes absolute freedom, trusting everyone to do what is right, and then degrading into a labyrinth of regulations for every behavior because people do not behave as they originally expected.

※

*When pride comes, then comes disgrace; but with the humble is
wisdom. (Prov. 11:2)*

This first part of this proverb brings to mind the adage "Pride comes
before the fall." Of course, this saying has roots in the story of Adam
and Eve, who committed the original sin and were cursed with pain
and death, along with being driven out of Paradise. This is such an
important lesson that it is repeated in Proverbs 18:16: "Pride goes
before destruction, and a haughty spirit before a fall." Warnings
against pride are common throughout the world, since pride is a vice
that no one likes in another person, but we are nearly always blind
to seeing it in ourselves. It is good, though, when people around us
are willing to point out our pride, arrogance, and hubris; this kind
of correction is part of love and friendship. At that point, we become able to understand the other problems in life that flow from
pride—especially the problems we blame on God, the world, and
everyone else.

This proverb speaks of disgrace, which is not merely a mistake
or an injury, but a public humiliation. It is not unusual to learn
of a wealthy businessman, an entertainment star, an athlete, or a
powerful politician being caught publicly in a scandal—what the
media often calls a "fall from grace." The disgraced figures typically
thought that they had it made and that they were indestructible,
so they took moral risks that eventually caught up to them. The
political commentator David Gergen famously said, "We have seen
the hubris; now come the scandals."

Nothing punctures the bubble of pride like a public mistake.
People can ignore and rationalize their private mistakes, but this
proverb reminds everyone that, ultimately, pride will expose them
to the scrutiny of others. The good news is that, when that happens, they might be properly humbled and accept proper correction.

Humbly accepting correction will remind the person that no one can manage all of life without the help of others and, more importantly, the grace of God. The wisdom of humility flows from knowing and accepting one's limits. No human can know everything, succeed in everything, do everything, or control everything. Humble acceptance of God's greatness and of the necessity of the rest of the people in the world is the wiser path to success for everyone involved.

I am very aware of this in my work and ministry. I have some facility with languages, and I can explain certain areas of philosophy and theology well enough, but I am a mathematical and mechanical moron. Furthermore, I am well aware that even in the areas of my academic strengths, I still need to learn from many teachers and books, and I still consult my friends to help me better understand the languages I have studied. I need experts in many fields, and I totally depend on the camera crews and staff who make possible the television shows I broadcast and the books I write. Without them, I could do very little, and I would embarrass myself if I tried to do it myself—and on television, no less!

Relying on other people for help is not weakness. Our culture is flat-out wrong when it tells us that the most important thing is to be totally independent; no one can live that way. We always need others, and so we should neither resent nor avoid asking for help. Since everyone is interdependent, neither should we resent being asked for help.

On the contrary, we can enjoy respecting and learning from the expertise of others as well as letting them use our own expertise. We rejoice for and with them that they excel in something different from what we are drawn to. The diversity of strengths and interests and talents with which humanity is blessed reflects God's goodness and love—and they make living together in society possible.

Sometimes this does not come easily for us, because some of us would like to take credit for being talented, good looking, intelligent, and so forth. Yet that attitude flows from human pride and arrogance, and it has to be undone. We can examine ourselves, see where we succeed and where we do not, and remember that God loves us with our own precise limitations—limitations that make all of us who we are. Our duty is to expand the abilities we possess, accept our limits, and use our talents and gifts for God's glory and for the service of others.

By insolence the heedless make strife, but with those who take advice is wisdom. (Prov. 13:10)

This proverb is a good follow-up to the last one. "Insolence" here could also be translated as "arrogance," and so again pride is connected to the inability to take guidance from others (or to take heed of their admonitions; that is the meaning of being "heedless"). But this time the proverb warns about the impact that such arrogance has not on ourselves, but on others.

The prideful person insists that he or she is right and will not take correction very well. The result is "strife"—unhelpful arguments that divide people, even friends. In these circumstances, it is important to know and accept the limits of our understanding—and to accept help from others. We can do well by getting a grasp on the things we do not know so that we can avoid the type of strife that is based on ignorance of the facts. So many arguments arise from insisting on some fact that turns out not to be the case. Not only is it embarrassing to get caught at arguing in favor of abject ignorance, but it can destroy friendships, families, and other relationships unnecessarily. Humility is our friend; insolent arrogance is our enemy and God's, too.

The name of the LORD *is a strong tower; the righteous man runs into it and is safe. (Prov. 18:10)*

How do we avoid pride? How do we stop thinking and acting as if we know it all and can do it all on our own according to the values and goals we set by ourselves for ourselves? How do we humble ourselves? The answer is easy to say, but hard to put into practice: we submit ourselves to the Lord. As this proverb says, He is a "strong tower" into which we run and in which we find refuge.

Humility does not mean deprecating ourselves, putting ourselves down, speaking badly about ourselves, and other such self-abasement. Notice that the focus remains as much on "ourselves" in each of those phrases as it does in the preceding paragraph. The very effort of putting ourselves down becomes an act of thinking about ourselves. Pride is a stance toward life from which we look down on others and consider ourselves more important than God or anyone else. Pride seeks to place the individual above everyone else; it enjoys being first, having more things, and being more important than others.

Pride, however, rarely takes pleasure in the objects and experiences that evoke it; the prideful person instead prefers the resulting feeling of superiority. The prideful enjoy being richer than anyone else rather than enjoying the money; they like recognition for owning something precious and rare rather than actually enjoying the rare item. They would rather speak about their self-importance in drinking the rarest wines or eating the best gourmet food rather than actually taste the delicacies. Some people will even try to boast about the ways in which they are more humble than everyone else—they even become proud of their "humility"! Most of them ignore the reality of the African proverb: the higher the monkey climbs, the greater the number of people who see his hind end.

Humility does not enjoy being superior to anyone else. The stance of humility is to look upward toward the infinite God. The humble person is aware that God is great and is the sole source of greatness. We neither exalt ourselves nor put ourselves down; we look to God, who is "a tower" infinitely higher than ourselves, our planet, and the universe itself.

The development of humility can begin by allowing the experience of wonder to overwhelm us when we see beautiful mountains, the ocean, the vastness of outer space, and the other beautiful wonders of nature. When we allow ourselves to admire and even be awestruck by beautiful art, scientific genius, magnificent buildings, and other goods fashioned by gifted people who use their talents to improve our world, then we learn humility. When we come to cherish beautiful and awe-inspiring realities, we cease to think about ourselves. As we think more deeply about these things, we want to search out the origin of the vastness and genius of the universe, or the inspiration for Michelangelo, Raphael, Bach, and other great artists. In that search beyond ourselves we come to understand that the Lord God is the ultimate source, the "strong tower" who eternally and infinitely pours out His abundance.

Since the name of the Lord is the "high tower," how do we run to His name in daily life and learn humility? As Catholics, whenever we pray, we always begin and end with the Sign of the Cross: "In the name of the Father, and of the Son, and of the Holy Spirit." With those simple words we run to Him—one God in three Persons. Also, we turn to Him in humility whenever we pray the Lord's Prayer, as seen in its opening words: "Our Father, who art in heaven, hallowed be thy name." By praying thoughtfully and sincerely in this way that God the Son taught us, we submit ourselves to the power of the Lord: "Thy will be done on earth as it is in heaven." We admit our smallness and that we cannot do it all or understand it all ourselves.

The last few words of this proverb could also be translated "set on high." So when we call upon God's name—when we belong to Christ and the Holy Spirit—He lifts us up. True exaltation doesn't come from the feeble, spindly kind of arrogance that we use to puff ourselves up. Rather, it comes from humbling ourselves before the Lord so that He can place us "on high."

The fear of the LORD is instruction in wisdom, and humility goes before honor. (Prov. 15:33)

The importance of fear of the Lord is a common theme throughout the book of Proverbs. We see elsewhere, for instance, that "the fear of the LORD is the beginning of knowledge" (Prov. 1:7) and "the fear of the LORD is the beginning of wisdom" (Prov. 9:10). The fear of the Lord is here identified as the attitude that makes "instruction in wisdom" possible. Fearing the Lord is a recognition that His will, particularly as expressed in His moral law, leads to instruction in wisdom. Recall that Moses had told the Israelites:

> Behold, I have taught you statutes and ordinances, as the LORD my God commanded me, that you should do them in the land which you are entering to take possession of it. Keep them and do them; for that will be your wisdom and your understanding in the sight of the peoples, who, when they hear all these statutes, will say, "Surely this great nation is a wise and understanding people." (Deut. 4:5–6)

God's statutes and laws are "wisdom" and "understanding," and the nation that fears the Lord will obey those laws and acquire their inherent wisdom and understanding by living in the moral way the Lord sets before people. His laws are not arbitrary expressions of some divine whim; rather, they speak of and promote the inherent good of the individual and of society as a whole.

We can then see the link between fear of the Lord and the "humility that goes before honor." We will see the value, truth, and goodness of God's law only if we are humble enough to accept His law on His terms. When we are humble enough to trust that obeying His law is good for us, and when we fear to break His law and to displease Him, then through this obedience we will become wise. Such humility will evoke the praise of other people, such as Moses had predicted, "Surely this great nation is a wise and understanding people." The wisdom of virtue will become apparent to us and to others, as we experience the peace of moral integrity. However, the proverbs assert that the opposite is true as well: "Before destruction a man's heart is haughty, but humility goes before honor" (Prov. 18:12).

This opposite parallel indicates that haughty pride is the contradiction of fear of the Lord. Therefore, the wise person chooses fear of the Lord and its consequent integrity and eschews arrogance. As a result, our virtue of humility will precede true honor, just as pride goes before a fall.

Where there is no guidance, a people falls; but in an abundance of counselors there is safety. (Prov. 11:14)

Many modern people view society as a collection of totally independent individuals going through life making their own decisions about moral issues as each of them sees fit. A popular image of the "good life" portrays it as limited by as few responsibilities to (and dependencies on) others as possible, while each individual maximizes pleasures and enjoyment. This proverb, however, strongly rejects that model of society for a more clearly interdependent one.

The first part of the proverb asserts that a people — that is, society — will fall if there is "no guidance" — no exchange of ideas or advice about the true good of the individual and the common good of all. The guidance, of course, draws upon the past experiences, both successes and failures, that make up the wealth of wisdom. Truly wise people adapt lessons from both good and bad experiences to present circumstances. This is why older people and those who study the past are treasure houses of guidance.

A sad phenomenon of the present use of social media is that children do not learn as much as they ought from their elders. They are so constantly attuned to their friends and peers through the various social media that they do not take the time to listen to the stories and lessons from those who aren't quite as Internet savvy. Professor Mark Bauerlein's excellent study *The Dumbest Generation* provides evidence that social media is a central culprit in the decline of knowledge among young people (and some older folks, too). Wise and knowledgeable people are better sources of social strength and wisdom than what is generally found in short, badly spelled tweets.

"There is safety" and security for a society in consultation and collaboration with the wise and intelligent. Humbling ourselves before the Lord and our fellow human beings who know more than we know or understand will strengthen society. Wisdom comes to us as it did for ancient Israel, the apostles, and the early Christians — as a community. By cultivating a spirit of humility and collaboration, we are more likely to make the Lord's guidance the first source of strength in our hearts, and the wisdom of others a source of strength for the whole culture.

CHAPTER 11

Silence and Speech

W e all know the childhood saying "Sticks and stones may break my bones, but words can never hurt me." Although this may reassure young people who are subjected to name calling, it does not mean that our words cannot have a negative impact on others and on ourselves. In this chapter, we'll look at the wisdom of the Proverbs on speech and silence.

The mouth of the righteous is a fountain of life, but the mouth of the wicked conceals violence. (Prov. 10:11)

Starting off on a positive note, the first part of this saying reminds us that good words are not idle but can be truly life-giving — well beyond what we can understand at the moment. The image for the verbal source of life is a spring of water. In ancient Israel, the life of an entire city would often depend on one natural fountain. Jericho has lasted for eleven thousand years, since the Neolithic Period, because of the Spring of Elisha, as it is known today, pouring out water for the whole Jericho oasis. Jerusalem has existed for more than five thousand years because of the Gihon Spring providing water since the Chalcolithic Period (ca. 3500 BC) and the Early Bronze Age (ca. 3000 BC), when the first buildings were constructed. Other cities — Megiddo, Gezer, Hazor, and others — also depended on a spring of water for their existence. Pilgrims still visit Mary's Well in Nazareth, which was the water source that made the village habitable. People who were absolutely dependent on settling near springs of water would consider applying this image to the "mouth of the righteous" a very powerful symbol for life.

Note also that the proverb contrasts the "mouth of the righteous" with the "mouth of the wicked," and not, for instance, the "mouth of the ignorant." This is a moral difference, not one of knowledge. While knowledge is important and extremely useful, the upright and moral use of it makes the difference between manufacturing tractors that help farmers grow food or tanks that kill enemies to ensure that the food reaches only one's friends and allies. Righteousness guides the physician to remove life-threatening cancer rather than take the life of an infant in the womb.

The moral difference between the righteous mouth and the wicked mouth naturally applies to the words that the person speaks to others. Wise and prudent words can bring comfort and peace to people struggling with anxiety or sin, or make sense out of their lives when they are faced with moral struggles or catastrophe. The words of the righteous can lead them to embrace Christ's life-giving love and forgiveness. We do well to pay close attention here to the seven Spiritual Works of Mercy, most of which are directly related to speech: instructing the ignorant, counseling the doubtful, admonishing sinners, bearing wrongs patiently, forgiving offenses willingly, comforting the afflicted, and praying for the living and the dead. Grace bubbles out—like a spring—from speech that serves God's will and brings truth and goodness to others, as well as to ourselves.

On the other hand, words that needlessly tear others down or spread falsehoods have incited violence throughout history. Karl Marx did very little by way of personal charity to relieve the pain and suffering of the working class, whose lives were truly miserable through the first century of the Industrial Revolution. In fact, he made the lives of his own family miserable by his neglect, if not actual abuse, and adultery. What he did instead was write many words that concealed violence very thinly. For instance, he viewed the development of modern industry as the means by which the bourgeoisie produces "its own grave-diggers" through the "inevitable" proletariat revolution (*Communist Manifesto*). He wrote that religion "is the opium of the people," and its abolition is the demand for the people's "real happiness" (*Critique of Hegel's Philosophy of Right*, 1843). These words inspired the Communist governments of the twentieth century who killed more than 150 million of their own citizens, including millions of Christians. Marx's wicked words concealed some of the most horrendous violence in history.

While Marx's words had an extremely wide influence on modern history, the rest of us can learn from that extreme: when our words are wicked, emerging from ill will and selfishness, they are capable of releasing evil effects we cannot anticipate or control. Our task is to be wise enough to speak words of righteousness that will bring peace and life not only to ourselves but to the world around us, perhaps even after we have died.

<hr />

Wise men lay up knowledge, but the babbling of a fool brings ruin near. (Prov. 10:14)

This proverb begins with wise people who "lay up," or store, knowledge. This is more than just collecting facts, as if preparing for a lifelong game of Trivial Pursuit or Jeopardy. Knowledge of the world is definitely a good in itself, but the knowledge of facts and data requires the wise person's ability to organize and interpret that information. Wisdom takes the facts of life and makes good sense of them. When knowledge has been organized through key concepts and ideas, people become capable of seeing patterns and insights that are useful for forming a coherent view of the world. The organization of the various facts of life will include God's revelation of truth in Sacred Scripture, the Sacred Tradition of the apostles, and the consistent Faith taught through the Magisterium.

This book is itself that kind of project; we have collected knowledge from the Scriptures, organized it thematically, and looked for patterns that will give us insights into life and faith. All people go through similar processes every day. When information appears to be useful, people want to remember it in order to use it in the future. For example, parents remember their children's responses to various disciplinary techniques, and spouses remember the effects their annoying habits have on their spouse. The organizing principles that underlie these remembered facts are the improvement of the children's behavior or the development of a better relationship with one's spouse. The same principle applies to all knowledge: people have certain goals and purposes that induce them to seek out some types of knowledge and remember them, while ignoring other things that seem irrelevant. The sage is the person who stores up and organizes the kinds of knowledge that are truly useful for living a good life with God and other people, both during this life and into eternity.

The "fool," on the other hand, speaks and acts without knowing much or without understanding why some knowledge is especially important, good, and true, while other knowledge is unhelpful. For instance, gossip, whether from Hollywood or from the neighborhood, is generally useless information. People who speak without knowledge of the facts tend to speak too much and too loudly as a way to cover up their ignorance. This is more than annoying when the babbling fool is in a position of authority, as in politics, punditry, or teaching. The wise person seeks to know much, to organize that knowledge wisely, and to speak with truth and moral righteousness.

———————————— ❧ ————————————

He who conceals hatred has lying lips, and he who utters slander is a fool. (Prov. 10:18)

Although the two parts to this proverb seem to be about different sins—hatred and slander—they actually are two sides of the same coin. The first part is a wise observation that makes a great deal of sense: to hide hatred or contempt for another person from others, we naturally have to say things about that person that we do not believe—or we are nice to that person's face but speak badly about him or her to others. Perhaps we tell ourselves that the purpose of the deceit is to preserve the other person's feelings, but often it just allows us to nurse our ill will longer. In this light, we can see that vices tend to compound one another—as when hatred leads to deceit.

The second part of the proverb teaches that speaking about our contempt or hatred in the form of gossip and slander is another form of evil. Slander spreads lies about other people, and detraction reveals information—false or true—that damages another person's reputation for no good reason. This is a form of gossip that has historically been considered a very serious sin, in part because it's so difficult to make right. Like falling dominoes or ripples in a pond, slander and detraction continue to spread out from the original source and can never be fully undone.

Wisdom frequently means remaining silent about things we know concerning another person. When it is prudent, we may go to the person ourselves and address the issue in a conversation. This can clear up the false elements of the slander and may help the person change the direction of his or her life for the better. Cruel rumors usually harden hearts and so do little good for anyone involved.

This saying is a warning against harboring hatred in our hearts and expressing it in our speech. Hatred in the heart tempts a person either to deceive others about it, or to commit the sins of slander or detraction. The solution is to be careful about our words, certainly, but first of all the lesson is to guard against the interior attitudes that breed hatred in our hearts.

The tongue of the righteous is choice silver; the mind of the wicked is of little worth. (Prov. 10:20)

There are two points in this proverb. First, speech that comes from a person living a Christ-centered life can be incredibly valuable, even more so than choice silver. Righteous speech can evangelize, spreading the Good News of forgiveness of sins, salvation, eternal life with God, and peace in the heart. Speech can point out the meaning and goodness of life and convince others to improve their lives. In everyday life—at school or the workplace or the grocery store—our words can witness to the goodness of the Catholic Faith. A little kindness here, a little word of encouragement there add up to a precious contribution to the lives of other people. Words are one of the primary ways we radiate the love of Christ.

Second, this proverb tells us just how corrosive wickedness is. Abandoning God cuts us off from the Truth, and so our minds wither. No doubt there are many very smart people who are also wicked, but in using that intelligence badly they have made it worthless—unless and until they turn back to the Lord and His righteousness. Sin corrupts every part of life; even the seemingly most precious part—the mind—is rendered worthless when we are separated from Him. But with Him, even the lowly tongue is like silver.

The lips of the righteous feed many, but fools die for lack of sense. . . . The words of the wicked lie in wait for blood, but the mouth of the upright delivers men. (Prov. 10:21; 12:6)

These proverbs teach about the power of good speech versus the power of wicked speech — more specifically, the power of speech in the hands of the good versus that power in evil hands. If there's one lesson that Proverbs wants us to take away about speech, it's that words never lack power.

The first saying here would have been particularly meaningful to ancient Israelites, who were largely a farming people. The kind but firm exhortations of a father or mother could motivate the family to the work needed to feed themselves and to make a living. And to this day, of course, the words of wise and good leaders can move many people to wise and good action — whether to prosperity or, as in the second proverb, to freedom.

From Abraham Lincoln to Dr. Martin Luther King Jr., and many others, history is full of people whose words have inspired and continue to inspire heroic action that leads to freedom and enhancement of the common good. That power to speak truth well is in all of us, with God's help. We don't have to be a powerful political figure to motivate a child to hard work and personal improvement, or to deliver a friend or relative from a sinful habit, such as drunkenness or drug use. Remember, from the very beginning of this chapter, the Spiritual Works of Mercy, each of which summons us to use speech to help and inspire others in ways that are precious to God.

Another consideration when we are facing those difficult situations when wise and prudent speech may be effective is the need first to spend time in prayer and meditation. Let us ask the Lord which words and phrases to use, what tone to take, and how to respond to the challenges we face. Such prayer is not some last-minute stop-gap measure, but rather a time of reflection and peace in the Lord's presence, seeking a wisdom that is beyond our immediate grasp. No one can plan ahead for the crises of life, but we can maintain our relationship with the Lord through constant prayer so that we are better able to handle the crises when they arrive.

Remember: the wicked and foolish people described in Proverbs rarely know they are wicked and foolish. The line between prudence and error is narrow and not always obvious; it is only through God's grace that we stay on the right side.

CHAPTER 12

Work and Idleness

Remarkably, so many of the realities described in the book of Proverbs in ancient times are still recognizable to people living two and a half millennia later. Some of the best examples are the sayings about hard work and the vice of sloth. They point to the timeless wisdom of this book—and of the consistency of human nature over the ages.

The Hebrew word for "lazy person," *atsal*, is often translated as "sluggard." Several proverbs hold the sluggard up for scorn. This criticism was especially important in ancient Israel because the whole community depended on hard work from each individual to cultivate land, harvest food, raise children, and so on. In modern times, only 2 percent of the population works in agriculture; not only do they feed the other 98 percent abundantly, but they provide enough food to export to other countries and to give away in charity. In ancient times, well over 90 percent worked in agriculture and the societies were rarely more than six weeks away from famine. Storage was limited, as were crop yields. Droughts and other natural catastrophes, plus war and brigandage, put all ancient populations at risk. As a result, everyone had to work very hard in order to survive, and there was little room for slacking off from necessary labor.

Yet even if modern society is not at risk as were the ancients, the lessons about the value of hard work remain as relevant as in the past, although in new and more technologically sophisticated ways.

———————⟐———————

Go to the ant, O sluggard; consider her ways, and be wise.
Without having any chief, officer or ruler, she prepares her food
in summer, and gathers her sustenance in harvest. (Prov. 6:6–8)

This proverb brings to mind other stories and sayings based on the behavior of animals from cultures around the world, such as Aesop's fables. Human observations of animal behavior often teach lessons about human behavior. The ant is a favorite example of industriousness, perhaps most famously in the fable of the ant and the grasshopper, in which the ant, which has stored up reserves for the winter, refuses to help the grasshopper, which has spent the entire summer singing. (Whether the fable also addresses the lack of generosity by the ant is still debated.)

The key point here is that the ant applies hard work and prudence without needing to be told by an authority figure to do so. Not only does the ant work hard without (apparent) supervision, but it appears to plan ahead by storing up food for the winter. The conclusion is that we should not have this type of prudent work ethic *only* when a boss, parent, or teacher is breathing down our necks. At some point in life, these people will not be present to tell us what to do. If we become dependent on authority for the most basic sustenance, it will be hard to be independent in anything else.

Another advantage of having a self-directed work ethic is the ability to pass down the good example of work and prudence to children and other students. Industrious adults are able to provide the necessities of life for those who cannot be independent — the young, the old, the infirm, and so on. Since society cannot function freely and healthily if most people need to be told to perform the basic duties of sustaining themselves, this proverb helps us see that freedom requires a self-directed work ethic. When someone does not work freely to maintain his existence, then a more dictatorial person will pick up the slack and enforce the steps needed to live. We would then be on the road to totalitarianism.

As a door turns on its hinges, so does a sluggard on his bed. (Prov. 26:14)

Some of us may find comfort in learning that the ancient Israelites turned over in their beds instead of waking up and jumping out to greet every day, just like many of us. They may not have had snooze buttons on an alarm, but just like you and me they were tempted to go back to sleep instead of getting up to face the day with eagerness and a big smile.

Of course, it is very important to get a good night's sleep; a lack of sleep over many years can be a contributing factor in the onset of Alzheimer's disease. While, on one hand, commercials enthusiastically promote labor-saving devices so that everyone can have more time for fun, on the other hand, our workaholic culture demands that people work more and sleep less in order to pay for those devices. Sleep deprivation is a common problem in America today, even though sleep and rest are essential to good health.

This proverb, however, admonishes the sluggard that too much sleep—or, more often, an unwillingness to get up promptly even when we get enough sleep—can negatively affect the entire day. Most of us can think back on days when we just sat around on the couch and then felt sluggish, even exhausted. Of course, rest is revitalizing, but too much rest can make us feel even more tired and lazy. During my lifetime the term "couch potato" was developed to describe this phenomenon. The phrase refers not only to the inactivity but the form of the bodies of those folks who consume prepared food that contributes less to their health than to their girth. Excitement over watching other people play sports replaces exercise and athletic activities with family and friends. The cliché of the young adult living in his parents' basement and playing video games and surfing the Internet in his underwear would be the poster boy for the sluggard of the ancient Proverbs.

The first conclusion to be drawn from this proverb is that it is time for the modern sluggard to shower, put on his clothes, think about the future, and find some kind of honest work. A key part of overcoming lazy behavior is to have a vision for one's future: What do I want for my life by the time I reach forty, fifty, retirement, and old age? What kind of house, vehicle, and style of life do I desire, and what do I have to do to reach that goal? What kind of family life do I want? Is life relegated to the basement as a cause of embarrassment to my parents a life goal? What do I want to give of myself to a spouse, or am I merely looking for a spouse who will make me look good and do the chores my parents do for me?

A deeper level of acquiring hope for the future is to ask: What does the Lord God want for me? What does our Lord Jesus want me to do for Him and for His Church? How might I contribute to helping the poor, the uneducated, or other suffering people? Taking time to pray and to listen to God speak to our hearts is necessary for us to hear God's "still, small voice" (1 Kings 19:12).

One of the most common reasons people give for not taking time to pray is that they do not have the time for it. Yet what about those five, or fifteen, or thirty minutes we spend lazily in bed in the mornings? I myself am not ready to face the day until I've spent at least an hour in prayer. I am constantly amazed at the way it seems that the Lord multiplies the minutes and hours of the day the way He multiplied the loaves and fish. The more time I spend in prayer, the more work I get done. Perhaps you are not comfortable praying for a full hour, but even if you begin with a few minutes of prayer in the morning, you will become more motivated to get going with the day after "a breakfast of grace" that can sustain you with the comfort of the Lord's presence and the strength of His vision and purpose for your life. Yes, prayer is one very good antidote to becoming a sluggard in the basement or a potato on the couch.

The sluggard says, "There is a lion outside! I shall be slain in the streets!" (Prov. 22:13)

Although lions had once roamed the land of Israel, they were not commonly found wandering the streets. This statement of the sluggard would be like someone in Chicago or New York claiming, "I can't go to work because there once were wolves roaming around here and I might get eaten!" This proverb is meant as a humorous saying to shame the sluggard into going to work. Underlying the saying is the reality that once a sluggard has become accustomed to laziness, he or she will grasp at any excuse to avoid labor.

Mother Angelica often spoke about our need to recover a "theology of risk." We might also call this a theology of trust — trust that the Lord is with us and that His Providence is always in charge, and so it is worth taking prudent risks. This was the guiding force behind Mother's founding and leadership of EWTN — "Unless you are willing to do the ridiculous, God will not do the miraculous." Of course, she was aware that some efforts might fail, but if the Lord had motivated her to try something that did not turn out as she had expected, she would wait and see what lesson or side effect might result even from the failure. Trusting our Lord Jesus and taking the risks He sets before us makes life an incredible adventure, and in the process, it forms us into saints. Mother Angelica also admitted to me privately, and later in public, "I have a lot of faith; my stomach just doesn't know it yet." She did feel anxiety and worry, but she let her faith and trust overcome those feelings as she continued to take risks for Jesus.

This principle applies to more than getting out of bed in the morning, though. Today's world is paralyzed by fear—fear of lawsuits, fear of judgment, fear of offense, fear of the politically incorrect, and so on. Sometimes these fears are legitimate, even if overblown. Others are like lions in the streets of Jerusalem—that is, nonexistent. Our task is to discern prayerfully among the fears and the risks we face, and then go out into the world with the confidence that comes only from the Lord and the graces He bestows upon us.

The way of a sluggard is overgrown with thorns, but the path of the upright is a highway. (Prov. 15:19)

This saying reveals the ultimate irony of sloth. While at the moment laziness may seem to be the easier, less trying path, in reality the preparation accomplished by hard work and foresight will make life easier and more enjoyable. In fact, laziness that fails to prepare one for life often leads to more and harder work in the future.

In ancient Israel they built embanked highways out of packed dirt in order to make transportation by foot, donkey, camel, or horse more efficient. For instance, the parable of the Good Samaritan took place on such a road, and Jesus rode into Jerusalem on a good packed-dirt road on Palm Sunday. The difficult work of building and maintaining such roads made it much easier to travel, and that is the image used in this proverb: in order to make some things in life easier, people have to do groundwork at the beginning.

Everyday life in the modern world is full of examples of the same realities. The student who regularly studies diligently does not have to stay up all night before an exam. The person who habitually cleans up around the house avoids the buildup of dirt and debris that eventually makes it more difficult to clean later. The parent who disciplines a child effectively as a youngster will not have to work as hard when the child's willpower and body grow stronger.

This proverb also applies in spiritual matters. Developing a virtue at an early stage of life is a lot easier than trying to develop that same habit when one is older. The reason is that bad habits are more ingrained in the older person and good habits take quite a bit longer to acquire. Regular prayer throughout every stage of one's life will make it easier to turn to God in a trial of temptation or suffering. Sanctity does not arise in a vacuum; it requires (sometimes challenging) spiritual groundwork. But that groundwork makes the path to Heaven so much clearer and more reachable, no matter how steep or narrow the path might be (see Matt. 7:13–14).

The desire of the sluggard kills him for his hands refuse to labor.
(Prov. 21:25)

We can have desires that push us forward on the path to sanctification, and we can have disordered desires that distract us from the work of growing in virtue, which is the work of everyday life. This proverb fits well in today's world. Think about people we know—perhaps even ourselves—who have been so distracted by desires for pleasure or entertainment that they even neglect their basic duties.

This saying is a reminder that disordered desires—that is to say, desires for sinful things or desires for acceptable things that are out of proportion to one's true needs—can become so extreme that a person can neglect his or her own well-being. This often manifests itself terribly in the various forms of addiction. The alcoholic or drug addict does not eat well, becomes unable to work, and destroys his or her family relationships, along with fouling the relationship with God. The gambler believes he or she can beat the "house" and win a fortune, even though the government allows the gambling company legally to rig the odds so that the house is assured of a profit at the gambling tables and machines. These and other addictions destroy the lives of the compulsive person unless he or she comes to accept the fact of powerlessness in the face of addiction and then turns to God, who is the only One powerful enough to overcome compulsions for alcohol, drugs, gambling, sex, food, shopping, and so on.

This proverb points out that such sinful attachments and addictions are nothing new. Modern society might be prone to particularly modern addictions, but the ancient Israelites also recognized that disordered desires are so controlling that they can become deadly. The ancients were people with the same human nature as we have, and they were beset by the same kinds of disordered and destructive addictions as we are. Our one great advantage, though, is Jesus Christ, whose Passion and Resurrection bought for us freedom from sin and the possibility of eternal life.

We can always turn to Him, especially recalling His Passion, when disordered desires threaten to sidetrack us from our duties. Just as He refused to drink the painkilling wine mixed with myrrh as He hung on the Cross (Mark 15:23), so can any addict find strength to overcome the substance that only *appears* to kill the pain, but in fact is the cause of greater pain and death. Jesus' ability to face His upcoming suffering while in Gethsemane and His embrace of dying for sinners, as well as His willingness to forgive both the Good Thief (Luke 23:39–43) and those who were jeering Him as He hung dying (Luke 23:34), should encourage us to face our weakness and inevitable death with hope and strength. He grants us the grace to say at every moment of life, "Father, into thy hands I commit my spirit" (Luke 23:46).

By seeking and accepting those graces from Jesus Christ we become capable of living life well, as God would have us live, in accord with our nature as creatures made in His image and likeness (Gen. 1:26–27). That is the deeper wisdom that God presents to those who would have life in abundance here on earth (John 10:10) and eternal life with God in Heaven.

ABOUT THE AUTHOR

Fr. Mitch Pacwa, S.J.

Fr. Mitch Pacwa, S.J., was born in Chicago in 1949. He entered the Society of Jesus in 1968, was ordained a priest in 1976, and continued his studies in Old Testament at Vanderbilt University, where he received his Ph.D. He taught Old and New Testaments and Hebrew for many years at universities and on EWTN. He began making programs at EWTN on February 29, 1984, because of which he jokingly describes himself as Mother Angelica's "Sadie Hawkins' Day date." He made numerous series on Sacred Scripture and then in January 2002 went to EWTN full time, hosting *EWTN Live*, *Threshold of Hope*, the Wednesday edition of the *Open Line* radio show, and many other programs. He has authored more than twenty books, mostly on Sacred Scripture.